FROM MORMON TO GOD 2

Excerpt from The Book Of Mormon:

*2 Nephi 29:6 "**Thou fool, that shall say: A Bible, we have got a Bible, and we need no more Bible**. Have ye obtained a Bible save it were by the Jews? 7. Know ye knot that there are more nations than one? Know ye not that I, the Lord your God, have created all men, and that I remember those who are upon the isles of the sea; and that I rule in the heavens above and in the earth beneath; and I bring forth my word unto the children of men, yea, even upon all the nations of the earth? 8 **Wherefore murmur ye, because that ye shall receive more of my word?** Know ye not that the testimony of two nations is a witness unto you that I am God, that I remember one nation like unto another? Wherefore, I speak the same words unto one nation like unto another. And when the two nations shall run together the testimony of the two nations shall run together also. 9 And I do this that I may prove unto many that I am the same yesterday, today, and forever; and that I speak forth my words according to mine own pleasure. And because that I have spoken one word ye need not suppose that I cannot speak another; **for my work is not yet finished; neither shall it be** until the end of man, neither from that time henceforth and forever.*

KJV Bible Excerpt: Galatians 1:8-9 "But though we, or an angel from heaven, preach any other gospel unto you than that which we have preached unto you, let him be accursed."

FROM MORMON TO GOD 2

"Heavy Doctrines Compared in Mormonism
and Christianity"

By KRISTEN HALE

IT IS FINISHED PRESS

It Is Finished Press
Visalia, CA 93292
559-571-2593
www.frommormontogod.com

It Is Finished Press
INDEPENDENT CHRISTIAN
PUBLISHER

To every Mormon who calls themselves a Christian- This book is for you, and will fill you with the most beautiful truth.

To every Christian entering evangelism- I pray this book gives you the right tools to reach Mormons around the World.

Excerpt from Joseph Smith:

"I have more to boast of than ever any man had. I am the only man that has ever been able to keep a whole church together since the days of Adam. A large majority of the whole have stood by me. Neither Paul the Apostle, John the Apostle, Peter the Apostle, nor Jesus Christ ever did it. I boast that no man ever did such a work as I. The followers of Jesus ran away from Him; but the Latter-day Saints never ran away from me yet."

Source: Joseph Smith himself, recorded in the History of the Church (Vol. 6, p. 408–409).

Acknowledgements

I'd like to sincerely thank my husband and my immediate family, as well as my Restoration family, for taking us in as their own. Your love will forever stand as a testimony of God's true grace and goodness. He shines through you all. To my three children, thank you for giving Mommy the time and space to write her second book. Your independence is shining, but more than that, you are steady, secure, and deeply loved by Your God and the village surrounding you.

To Bishop Robert Hooks, thank you for your encouragement and for leading such a powerful, Spirit-filled ministry. It is an absolute privilege to be a member and a small part of what God is doing through Restoration Ministry church.

To Mom Trish, thank you for praying me through the battles that came with writing this book. Your timely intercession has carried me.

And above all, I thank my Lord and Savior, Jesus Christ, for Loving me, for saving me, for supplying me with His own wisdom, His truth, and His love. It is true—the truth really does set us free!

TABLE OF CONTENTS

Foreword

In a world where doubt and uncertainty can challenge our beliefs, the author of this book has courageously embraced a new faith. Kristen's journey from Mormonism to orthodox Christianity is a testament to her unwavering commitment to seeking truth and understanding scripture on a deeper level. Her story is one of resilience, faith, and a steadfast devotion to God that will inspire all who read it. Having had the privilege of knowing Kristen, her husband, Jeff, and their children, it is evident that Kristen's quest for answers is rooted in a heart full of compassion. Kristen's narrative is not one of animosity towards the Mormon faith; rather, it is a testament to her love for the congregation and her family. I deeply admire her unique, authentic approach in sharing her discoveries about the nature of Jesus Christ and the purpose of salvation based on biblical truths. These revelations have truly set her free.

Robert E. Hooks
Lead Pastor, Restoration Ministry Visalia, California

Preface

Mormons are some of the kindest people I've ever met. I was one of them for 27 years until a life-altering illness brought me to the real Jesus, and He delivered me. I am so grateful. I write these chapters with love and compassion for the Mormon people. I am not attacking them, I'm comparing scripture. I'm so grateful God brought me the truth and I want to share it with everyone I love so deeply.

Jesus is the Word and the Creator. Everything exists because of Him. He alone is God above all gods, our source of life, love, and strength. Scripture calls us to love Him first, because without loving Him we cannot truly love anyone else.

We need faith, not in ourselves, but in the grace God already gave 2,000 years ago.. Faith isn't a feeling or willpower; God Himself is the author and finisher of our faith (Hebrews 12:2). "Without faith it is impossible to please God" (Hebrews 11:6, NIV). His name, Jesus, still moves mountains.

You see, people need an anchor. They need a God who doesn't lie, who stays the same, who keeps His word. "God is not a man, that He should lie" (Numbers 23:19, KJV). He is perfect. He carried what we could never carry on the cross. It is finished.

Scripture teaches that salvation is a gift of grace, not something we earn (Ephesians 2:8–9). Jesus didn't just open a door for us to prove our worthiness; He is the Way (John 14:6).

Mormon doctrine teaches that Jesus' death simply gave us "agency" so we can save ourselves through works, ordinances, and worthiness, but the Bible teaches that salvation is entirely Christ's finished work.

Mormon temples, garments, and tithing interviews are presented as sacred, but they function more like a religious system than the gospel. Jesus warned of outward displays of righteousness (Matthew 23:5, NLT). God looks at the heart. I'm so grateful to be set free from religious systems, and into the loving arms of grace.

John 3:16 says, "whoever believes in Him," not "whoever wears the right garments," "goes to the temple," or "pays tithing perfectly." Works follow salvation—they don't create it (James 2:17; Hebrews 10:10). We obey because we have been saved, not to become saved.

Mormonism minimizes the cross and centers salvation on resurrection and personal effort. But "the message of the cross… is the power of God" (1 Corinthians 1:18). Jesus died not to give us agency—we already had that—but to give us eternal life.

I understand that speaking plainly may be viewed as "contention" in Mormon culture, where questioning doctrine is often discouraged. But Jesus said He came not to bring peace, but a sword (Matthew 10:34)—not to harm, but to divide truth from error. My intent is to speak the truth in love (Ephesians 4:15), because without love, our words mean nothing (1 Corinthians 13:1).

Biblical love is not soft, it is sacrificial: "There is no greater love than to lay down one's life" (John 15:13). Jesus laid His life down willingly (John 10:18, NIV; NLT).

That is the gospel. Mormon works and ordinances cannot add to what He already finished.

The old system of laws and rituals has been set aside as "weak and useless" (Hebrews 7:18, NLT). Satan has kept many in bondage by clinging to Old Testament law while skipping the New Testament, replacing it with *The Book of Mormon*, a "different gospel" Scripture warns about (Galatians 1:8, NLT). However, the apostles preached forgiveness and justification through Jesus alone (Acts 13:38–39). Jesus fulfilled the Law and the Prophets (Matthew 5:17, NLT). The Greek word for "fulfill" means to complete, render full. That's why His final words were, "It is finished" (John 19:30, NIV).

You may remember from Book 1 how God healed me of POTS, an "incurable" heart and neurological disease. If you haven't read it yet, I encourage you to read Book 1 first if you'd like to hear my testimony of what God did for me. This book (book 2) will go deeper. <u>We will compare the major doctrines of Mormonism and Christianity</u>, and it will be heavier than the first book.

God has made it clear to me that Book 2 is needed—especially for those leaving Mormonism. He loves every person, but we only become His children when we are born again.

"Yet to all who did receive Him, to those who believed in His name, He gave the right to become children of God." (John 1:12, NIV)

Mormonism teaches that all humans are automatically God's children. Scripture says otherwise. Becoming God's child is a right given only to those who believe.

I'm praying even now for those trapped in false systems, Mormonism, <u>or any man-made religion</u>, that God will give me clarity, wisdom, and courage to speak truth. What follows may stir "contention," something forbidden in Mormon culture, but truth often does.

"So then, have I become your enemy by telling you the truth?"

(Galatians 4:16, ASV)

I am in no way harassing Mormons. I'm simply unable to deny the truth Jesus showed me. If the LDS Church sends out over 100,000 missionaries each year to proclaim their message, then I, just one woman, can surely proclaim the good news of Christ. And I will, for the rest of my life.

Introduction

There is Christ's Gospel, and then there is "another gospel," the very thing Paul warned against in Galatians 1:8. *The Book of Mormon* openly calls itself "Another Testament of Jesus Christ," which places it exactly in the category Paul cautioned the Galatians about.

To avoid confusion in this book, anything quoted from the Mormon "another gospel" will be *italicized* so the contrast between Christ's Gospel and the *LDS version* is unmistakable. The word gospel in Greek means "good news." But *Mormonism* does not bring good news, only the heavy burden of works, worthiness, and a condemning, man-made "god."

As Pastor Rick Cardoso of Golden Grain Bible College once said, "When you read the Bible, mere knowledge does not save you. Belief does. Faith does" (teaching from Romans 5).

This book is about Scripture, defending the Word of God while contrasting it with Mormon doctrines and ordinances that directly oppose it. God exalts His Word above His own name (Psalm 138:2). If you have the wrong words, you end up with the wrong god.

This book is placed in no particular order, pick and choose the topic you'd like to learn about today, and allow God to rewire the activity in your brain. Chew on it, meditate on it, and learn something GOOD and NEW.

Those who are entering evangelism, may this book be used as a tool for you to reach Mormons around the world.

THE WORD

John opens his Gospel by revealing who Jesus truly is: "In the beginning the Word already existed. The Word was with God, and the Word was God" (John 1:1, NLT). This "Word" is not an idea or a message, it is Christ Himself. John clarifies: "So the Word became human and made his home among us" (John 1:14, NLT). Jesus is God in the flesh, "Emmanuel"=God with us (Matthew 1:23; cf. Isaiah 7:14, NLT).

The Gospel is simple and powerful: the eternal Word entered the world through the virgin Mary by the Holy Spirit, died for our sins, and rose again. Scripture teaches that without the shedding of blood there is no forgiveness (Hebrews 9:22, NLT). Christ's sacrifice was completed on the cross, not in Gethsemane. His suffering in the garden was real, but the atonement required death, not sweat. The cross is the center of salvation: "The message of the cross… is the power of God" (1 Corinthians 1:18, NLT).

Jesus laid His life down willingly: "No one can take my life from me. I sacrifice it voluntarily" (John 10:18, NLT). Salvation is fully His work. He declared, "It is finished!" (John 19:30, NLT). We are saved by grace through faith, not by human worthiness or effort (Ephesians 2:8–9, NLT). Works follow salvation, they never create it.

The Mormon LDS Joseph Smith Translation alters John 1:1 to read:

"In the beginning was the gospel preached through the Son…" (JST, John 1:1).

This shifts the meaning entirely, from Jesus Himself being the eternal Word, to "the gospel" being a message preached by the Son. It is an added interpretation, not found in biblical manuscripts. This alteration creates confusion about Christ's identity and undermines the plain testimony of Scripture.

MORMONISM

Mormon doctrine further teaches that Christ's atonement began, and in large part occurred in Gethsemane (*Book of Mormon, Mosiah 3:7; Doctrine and Covenants 19:18*). The Bible never teaches this. Scripture is consistent: the atoning sacrifice was His death, His shed blood, at Calvary.

Mormon LDS theology also teaches that Jesus' death primarily restored "agency," enabling people to earn exaltation through ordinances, temple rituals, and worthiness requirements. This stands in direct contradiction to the biblical teaching that Christ completed the work entirely.

Many raised in Mormonism struggle to accept unconditional love because LDS doctrine ties salvation to effort, performance, and obedience to thousands of rules. But Christ accomplished what no human could. Salvation is not earned, it is received.

He did all the work.It is finished.

FREE WILL

From the beginning, Adam and Eve were created with free will, image-bearers capable of choosing obedience or rebellion. Their decision to eat from the forbidden tree was an exercise of that God-given freedom. Long before humanity's fall, angels also possessed this capacity. Lucifer used his freedom to exalt himself in pride, and as a result, he "fell from heaven like lightning," as Jesus described (Luke 10:18, NLT).

Free will, misused by both mankind and angels, opened the door for sin to enter the world. Yet Scripture is clear: sin itself is condemned. Through His death and resurrection, Christ "condemned sin in the flesh" and disarmed its power for all who belong to Him (Romans 8:3, NLT).

Some point to Jesus' words in John 15:16 "You didn't choose me. I chose you" (NLT), as if they contradict human freedom. But He was speaking directly to His disciples, whom He appointed for a unique and specific ministry. This passage does not negate human free will; it highlights divine calling for service.

Here is the essential truth: Jesus did not die to give humanity free will. Free will already existed, from creation, and even before creation in the angelic realm. Jesus died to conquer sin and death. He went into the grave, took the keys of death and hell, and rose victorious on the third day. Through faith in Him, we receive eternal life (John 3:16, NLT). That is the true purpose and power of the cross.

MORMONISM

Mormon LDS doctrine teaches that one purpose of Jesus' atonement was to restore or secure human "agency." The Book of Mormon states that humans "are free to choose liberty and eternal life" because of the Messiah (2 Nephi 2:27, Book of Mormon). LDS leaders frequently describe "the gift of agency" as something tied directly to Christ's atonement.

However, this creates a theological contradiction:

If Adam, Eve, and even Lucifer already exercised free will, then agency did not originate from Christ's atonement. In the biblical worldview, agency predates human history. But in LDS teaching, Jesus becomes the giver of free will rather than the Redeemer who conquers sin.

According to the Bible, Jesus frees us from sin, not into agency, because agency was already present. The LDS redefinition shifts the focus of the cross away from redemption and toward the preservation of free will. This reduces Jesus to a facilitator of choice rather than the Savior who delivers from death.

Biblically, Jesus' mission was clear: to save sinners, destroy the works of the devil, and grant eternal life through faith. Any teaching that assigns Him a different purpose becomes, by definition, another gospel.

JESUS IS GOD

CHRISTIANITY

Scripture reveals one God who exists eternally in three persons: the Father, the Son, and the Holy Spirit. God the Father is spirit (John 4:24, NLT) and invisible (1 Timothy 1:17, NLT). Jesus Christ is fully God and fully man, united with the Father in essence. The Holy Spirit is fully God, the indwelling presence of God in believers.

Paul writes, "For in Christ lives all the fullness of God in a human body" (Colossians 2:9, NLT). Jesus is not part of God; He is fully God in bodily form. This aligns with Israel's confession: "Listen, O Israel! The Lord is our God, the Lord alone" (Deuteronomy 6:4, NLT). God is one in essence.

The Lord declares, "Before me there was no God formed, nor will there be one after me" (Isaiah 43:10, NLT). Scripture leaves no room for multiple gods, exalted beings, or divine progression. There is only one eternal God.

Jesus speaks of this unity in His prayer: the Father is in the Son, the Son is in the Father, and believers are brought into fellowship with God through faith (John 17:21–23, NLT). We are saved because the perfect God redeems imperfect people, not because we can ever rise to His level.

Christians throughout history have used illustrations to grasp this mystery. St. Patrick taught the Trinity using a shamrock: three leaves, one clover. Others have used an egg or three candles forming one flame. These are limited pictures, but they point us toward the truth that God is three in person, one in nature—a truth the natural mind cannot grasp without the Spirit (2 Corinthians 4:3–4, NLT).

When we receive Jesus, God Himself dwells in us (John 1:12, NLT). Jesus is Emmanuel, "God with us", fully human and fully divine.

MORMONISM

Mormonism teaches something fundamentally different: not one God in three persons, but three separate gods united only in purpose.

LDS doctrine states: God the Father (Heavenly Father) is an exalted man with a physical, glorified body, Jesus is a separate god, also with a physical body, who became divine through obedience, The Holy Ghost is a separate being, a spirit without a body (Gospel Principles manual; Teachings of Joseph Smith).

Mormon Doctrine and Covenants 130:22 reads:

"The Father has a body of flesh and bones as tangible as man's; the Son also; but the Holy Ghost… is a personage of Spirit."

Mormon Latter Day Saint teaching also holds that God the Father is one among many gods who were once mortal and were exalted. Humans may follow this same path and *"become gods"* through obedience and temple ordinances (*D&C 132:19-20*).

This system is not the biblical Trinity. It is not one God in three persons. It is three separate gods, each with a different nature and origin. Mormonism does not affirm that Jesus is eternally God.

The Bible does.

These are two entirely different understandings of who God is, and two incompatible gospels.

FATHER OF THE COVENANT

CHRISTIANITY

In Scripture, Abraham stands as the foundational covenant father. God Himself identifies as "the God of Abraham, Isaac, and Jacob" (Exod. 3:6, NLT). Abraham is the man through whom God established a covenant that shaped all redemptive history.

God called Abram out of his country and promised to make him "a great nation" (Gen. 12:2, NLT). When Abram believed God, "the LORD counted him as righteous because of his faith" (Gen. 15:6, NLT). Later, God sealed this covenant by changing Abram's name to Abraham, meaning "father of many nations" (Gen. 17:5, NLT), and Sarai's name to Sarah (Gen. 17:15, NLT). The inserted "H" carries the breath of God, marking divine covenant participation (Garlow & Price, 2013).

Abraham's obedience is most clearly shown when God commanded him to offer Isaac, the son of promise, on Mount Moriah. Abraham trusted that God would provide, and God indeed stopped him, declaring, "Now I know that you truly fear God" (Gen. 22:12, NLT). This moment foreshadowed the greater reality of the Father offering His only Son, Jesus Christ, for our salvation.

Through Christ, believers become true children of Abraham by faith: "And because we are his children, God has sent the Spirit of his Son into our hearts, prompting us to call out, 'Abba, Father'" (Gal. 4:6, NLT). The Abrahamic covenant is fulfilled in Christ alone, and only those united to Christ share in it.

MORMONISM

In *Mormon* scripture, the role that Scripture gives to Abraham is overshadowed by Lehi, presented as the spiritual and patriarchal father of Book of Mormon peoples. Lehi is described as a prophet who receives visions, dreams, and warnings before fleeing Jerusalem to establish a new covenant lineage (1 Nephi 1–2). His son Nephi records these revelations and treats Lehi as the origin point of a new chosen branch of Israel (more in next chapter).

The Book of Mormon positions *Lehi*, not Abraham, as the functional covenant father for its narrative. While the text occasionally references Abraham, its covenant identity centers on Lehi's family receiving promises of land, prosperity, and divine favor (*1 Nephi 2:19–24*). The storyline develops an alternate lineage that claims prophetic authority apart from the biblical covenant established through Abraham.

Because of this, Mormon doctrine does not ground its identity in being children of Abraham by faith in Christ. Instead, LDS teaching emphasizes belonging to covenant "tribes" through patriarchal blessings, lineage assignments, and Book of Mormon ancestry rather than the biblical connection to Abraham, Isaac, and Jacob.

This shift replaces the singular, God-ordained covenant line with a new prophetic origin unique to *LDS scripture*. As a result, the biblical meaning of being God's children, those who cry out "Abba, Father" through the Spirit, is redefined in LDS theology through lineage, works, and institutional belonging rather than through faith in Christ alone.

DESTRUCTION OF JERUSALEM

CHRISTIANITY

The destruction of Jerusalem, as depicted in the Bible through the prophet Jeremiah, is a deeply mournful event. Jeremiah prophesied for more than forty years, warning the people of Judah about their impending doom due to their wickedness, idolatry, and rejection of God's call to repentance. His sorrow is vividly expressed in the book of Lamentations, where he laments the fall of the city and the suffering of its people. The Bible paints a picture of a city filled with corrupt leadership, defiant citizens, and spiritual decay, leading to its eventual destruction by the Babylonians in 586 BCE. As recorded in 2 Kings 25 and Jeremiah 39, after the Babylonians breached the city's walls, they destroyed the temple, burned the royal houses, and took the people into captivity. Jeremiah himself, though spared from captivity, mourned not just the physical destruction but the spiritual downfall of Jerusalem.

MORMONISM

In stark contrast, the *Book of Mormon* presents a different narrative of Jerusalem's destruction. Mormon prophet *Lehi*, said to be living in Jerusalem around 600 BCE, is warned by God to flee the city BEFORE the destruction, driven by a vision and divine command. The Book of Mormon recounts how *Lehi*, with his family and a few others, escape into the wilderness to avoid the consequences of Jerusalem's wickedness (as if you can escape God's judgement.) *Lehi's* flight marks the beginning of the Book of Mormon, where his descendants, the *Nephites and Lamanites*, establish their own civilizations.

This narrative differs from the Bible's account, where there is no mention of a select group fleeing prior to the destruction. Instead, the Bible stresses the collective consequences of disobedience, with no hint of a miraculous or preemptive escape like that of *Lehi's* family.

TOWER OF BABEL

CHRISTIANITY

Scripture presents the Tower of Babel as a unified human effort rooted in pride rather than faith. After the flood, humanity shared one language and one purpose. Instead of spreading across the earth as God commanded, they sought to make a name for themselves by building a tower that would reach the heavens (Genesis 11:1–4, NLT). This project was not about worship but self-exaltation, humanity attempting to ascend to God on its own terms.

God intervened mercifully and decisively. He confused their language, causing them to stop building and disperse over the earth (Genesis 11:5–9, NLT). The confusion of languages was not arbitrary punishment but divine restraint, preventing unchecked human pride and preserving God's redemptive plan. Scripture later affirms that God alone determines how He is approached and revealed, and warns clearly against adding to His revealed word (Deuteronomy 4:2; Proverbs 30:5–6; Revelation 22:18–19, NLT). The Babel account stands as a boundary marker: human effort cannot bridge the gap to God, and God's revelation is complete and guarded.

MORMONISM

The Book of Mormon teaches that during the Tower of Babel, God preserved the language of the brother of

Jared's family, allowing them to remain unified while others were confused (Ether 1:33–37). This exception is absent from the biblical account. By introducing a preserved lineage and language, the Book of Mormon adds to an event the Bible presents as universal and complete, standing in tension with Scripture's explicit warning not to add to God's word (15 more parallel stories just like these are listed at the end of the book).

MONOTHEISM VS POLYTHEISM

CHRISTIANITY

Christian faith begins with the unshakable confession that God is one. Scripture declares, "Hear, O Israel! The Lord is our God, the Lord alone" (Deut. 6:4, NLT). God is not one among many; He is the only eternal Creator. The Lord Himself affirms, "I am the first and the last; there is no other God" (Isa. 44:6, NLT). He further declares, "I alone am God… No one can take you out of my hand" (Isa. 43:13, NLT).

This one God, Father, Son, and Holy Spirit, is one Being in three co-equal persons, not three gods, but one divine essence revealed relationally and eternally. The Son is fully God (John 1:1, NLT), and the Spirit is fully God (Acts 5:3–4, NLT), yet Scripture never divides the Godhead into separate beings. The Lord alone created the heavens and the earth, acting without assistance from any other deity: "By my hands I stretched out the heavens; all the stars are at my command" (Isa. 45:12, NLT). Creation is the work of the one sovereign God who shaped the world for His image-bearers, Adam and Eve, so they might live under His care and reflect His glory.

The biblical witness is consistent from Genesis to Revelation: there was no God before Him, and there will be none after Him. God is eternally unique, self-existent, and without peers, rivals, or predecessors. Christian doctrine stands firmly on this foundation, one God, eternally God, alone God.

MORMONISM

In *Mormon Latter-day Saint* doctrine, God is not understood as the only eternal being or the sole Creator. The Book of Abraham presents a scene in which multiple gods participate in the creation, using the repeated phrase, "the Gods" (Abraham 4–5, Pearl of Great Price). The Mormon temple confirms "Michael" as another creator, later turned into Adam. Doctrine and Covenants teaches that there are "worlds without number" created (D&C 76:24; 93:10), and that these creations involve divine beings beyond the Father alone. LDS leaders frequently interpret the plural "we" in their scriptures to indicate cooperation among distinct gods who share a hierarchy within what they call the "Godhead."

Latter-day Saint theology further holds that God the Father was once a man who progressed to godhood and that faithful humans may also become exalted to create worlds of their own. As Lorenzo Snow famously summarized, "As man now is, God once was; as God now is, man may be." This concept affirms a cosmos populated with many gods, many worlds, and many divine offspring, an eternal chain of exalted beings extending into eternity.

While Christianity proclaims one God who alone is Creator, Mormonism presents a divine community of separate gods, each capable of advancement and creation. This difference is not minor but foundational. The biblical vision anchors salvation in the eternal, unchanging God; Mormon doctrine builds its hope on a progression toward becoming a god. The contrast is therefore unmistakable: one God from everlasting to everlasting in Scripture, and many gods of varying authority in LDS belief.

DON'T ADD

CHRISTIANITY

Biblical Scripture is clear: God's Word is pure, sufficient, and not to be altered.

Psalm 12:6 declares, "The Lord's promises are pure, like silver refined in a furnace, purified seven times" (NLT).

Paul affirms that "All Scripture is inspired by God and is useful to teach us what is true… God uses it to prepare and equip his people to do every good work" (2 Tim. 3:16–17, NLT).

Hebrews reminds us that God's Word is "alive and powerful… cutting between soul and spirit… exposing our innermost thoughts and desires" (Heb. 4:12, NLT). And God's command is unmistakable: "Do not add to or subtract from these commands I am giving you" (Deut. 4:2, NLT). Proverbs offers the same warning: "Do not add to his words, or he may rebuke you and expose you as a liar" (Prov. 30:6, NLT).

The final warning of Scripture is sobering: "If anyone adds anything… God will add to that person the plagues described in this book. And if anyone removes any of the words… God will take away that person's share in the tree of life" (Rev. 22:18–19, NLT).

Jesus Himself demonstrated the authority and sufficiency of Scripture. When tempted in the wilderness

(Matt. 4:1–11), He did not debate Satan, He simply wielded Scripture. He quoted Deuteronomy to cut through every lie (Deut. 8:3; 6:13; 6:16). If the Son of God relied on the written Word, we must do the same.

The Bible does not need to be corrected, improved, or added to. It stands complete and authoritative.

MORMONISM

In contrast, *Mormonism* openly introduces an additional book of scripture. The Book of Mormon calls itself "Another Testament of Jesus Christ," which directly conflicts with the biblical command not to add to God's Word, as said above.

LDS members are taught from childhood that the Bible is reliable only *"as far as it is translated correctly" (Articles of Faith 1:8)*. This single phrase plants lifelong doubt, allowing any biblical passage that contradicts Mormon doctrine to be dismissed.

This creates a built-in shield against the true Gospel. When the Bible disagrees with Mormonism, the Bible is blamed, not the doctrine. Many are also taught that the Joseph Smith Translation (JST) is the "correct" version of Scripture, even though it contradicts the original text and conveniently supports LDS teachings.

The result is a system where trust in the Bible is undermined before a child can even read it. The problem is not that Scripture is corrupted, the problem is that hearts and minds have been trained to question the very foundation of God's Word.

The Bible's warnings are not optional. Adding to Scripture or elevating another gospel places a person in spiritual danger (Rev. 22:18–19). The Word of God stands alone, complete and sufficient. Anything added beside it or above it is a distortion, not truth.

THE SECOND COMING

CHRISTIANITY

Scripture gives a clear picture of the Second Coming of Jesus Christ. Paul writes that Jesus will return "with his mighty angels, in flaming fire, bringing judgment on those who don't know God and on those who refuse to obey the Good News" (2 Thess. 1:7–8, NLT). Those who reject Him will face "eternal destruction, forever separated from the Lord" (2 Thess. 1:9–10, NLT).

Revelation describes this return with unmistakable imagery: Christ comes on a white horse, His eyes like flames, His robe dipped in blood, and His name declared, "King of Kings and Lord of Lords" (Rev. 19:11–16, NLT). Jesus also taught that He will come with His angels in glory (Matt. 25:31, NLT).

One of the clearest summaries is found in Hebrews: "Christ… will appear a second time, not to deal with sin, but to bring salvation to all who are eagerly waiting for him" (Heb. 9:28, NLT). His first coming dealt with sin once for all (Heb. 10:10); His second coming completes redemption for those who already belong to Him.

At His ascension, angels affirmed the manner of His return: "This same Jesus… will return from heaven in the same way you saw him go" (Acts 1:11, NLT). The Bible does not indicate additional bodily visitations between His ascension and His final return.

While Christ appears in visions or heavenly glory (Acts 7; 9; 18; Rev. 1), Scripture never describes Him physically walking the earth again before His Second Coming. His one future return remains decisive and final.

Forgiveness and salvation are available now, not at the Second Coming. Believers are justified fully through Christ's finished work: "For by that one offering he forever made perfect those who are being made holy" (Heb. 10:14, NLT).

Salvation is complete in Him alone: "Apart from me you can do nothing" (John 15:5, NLT).

And He Himself declared, "It is finished!" (John 19:30, NLT).

MORMONISM

Mormon doctrine teaches that after His ascension, Jesus Christ physically visited the Americas (*Book of Mormon, 3 Nephi 11–28)*. This claim conflicts with the angelic declaration in Acts 1:11 that Christ will return in the same way He ascended, once, visibly, and in glory. A bodily appearance in the Americas prior to His Second Coming alters the biblical timeline and minimizes the finality of His promised return.

Mormon LDS teachings also differ in their understanding of forgiveness. Instead of salvation being complete through Christ's finished work, Mormonism teaches that forgiveness is conditional and ongoing. Children are considered sinless until age 8. At baptism, sins before age 8 are washed away, but afterward forgiveness depends on continual repentance and obedience to LDS ordinances (Book of Mormon, Moroni 8; Doctrine and Covenants 20).

In *Mormon Latter Day Saint* doctrine, full forgiveness is ultimately connected to Christ's return and personal worthiness. They teach a multi-stage afterlife: spirit paradise and spirit prison, missionary work among the dead, and the possibility of progressing through kingdoms of glory before the final judgment. Temples are believed to remain on earth during Christ's return so proxy ordinances for the dead can continue.

This stands in direct contrast to Scripture, which teaches that the day of the Lord will bring final judgment: "The earth and everything on it will be found to deserve judgment" (2 Pet. 3:10, NLT), and "the first heaven and the first earth had disappeared" (Rev. 21:1, NLT). No ongoing temple work or second chances are described.

Most importantly, Mormon doctrine denies the complete and finished forgiveness available now through Christ alone. Scripture teaches that believers already stand forgiven, perfected, and complete because of Christ's sacrifice, not because of ongoing works or future cleansing.

The Gospel calls every person to receive salvation today, not at His return: "How can they believe in him if they have never heard about him? And how can they hear about him unless someone tells them?" (Rom. 10:14, NLT). Christ saves fully now, by grace through faith.

PEACE

CHRISTIANITY

Jesus promises a peace the world cannot give, peace that holds in the middle of storms, not merely after they pass. He told His disciples, "Here on earth you will have many trials and sorrows. But take heart, because I have overcome the world" (John 16:33, NLT). Our peace is rooted in who He is, not in our ability to endure.

When the disciples panicked during a violent storm on the Sea of Galilee, Jesus asked them, "Why are you afraid? Do you still have no faith?" (Mark 4:40, NLT). Their fear showed how quickly we forget that God is present even when the waves rise. True faith learns to trust in the storm, not only after the storm.

Scripture consistently directs us away from anxiety and toward trust. "Don't worry about anything; instead, pray about everything… Then you will experience God's peace" (Phil. 4:6–7, NLT). Jesus also said, "Don't worry about tomorrow" (Matt. 6:34, NLT). When we seek God's kingdom first, "all these things will be added to you" (Matt. 6:33, NLT).

God is trustworthy. He listens, protects, comforts, and carries our burdens. Anxiety may come, but His strength meets us in our weakness. "My grace is all you need. My power works best in weakness" (2 Cor. 12:9, NLT). Jesus also promised, "I am leaving you with a gift, peace of mind and heart" (John 14:27, NLT).

In every temptation or trial, God is faithful: "He will show you a way out so that you can endure" (1 Cor. 10:13, NLT). The emphasis is on His faithfulness, not our personal stamina. Peace is not a prize at the end of a trial. Peace is the presence of God in the trial.

MORMONISM

Mormonism presents a fundamentally different pattern. In LDS scripture, peace and salvation come <u>after</u> human endurance:

- *"He that endureth to the end, the same shall be saved... unless a man shall endure to the end... he cannot be saved." (2 Nephi 31:15–16)*
- *"Unto him that endureth to the end will I give eternal life." (3 Nephi 15:9)*

Mormon salvation is conditioned on man's ability to persist faithfully. *Mormon god's* peace is offered only when the trial has been endured successfully.

Mormon Doctrine and Covenants reinforces this:

"Peace be unto thy soul; thine adversity... shall be but a small moment; and then, if thou endure it well, God shall exalt thee on high." (D&C 121:7–8)

This is an if/then system:

If you endure well, <u>then</u> you may receive peace and exaltation.

The focus is on human performance, your endurance, your worthiness, your obedience.

Similarly, *Mormon Ether 12:6 teaches:*

"Ye receive no witness until after the trial of your faith."

And *Mormon Ether 12:27* links God's grace to personal humility and faithful performance:

"...if they humble themselves before me... then will I make weak things become strong."

These passages create a perpetual "almost-there" spirituality. Peace is held just out of reach until the believer proves themselves worthy through endurance. LDS doctrine reinforces this idea repeatedly, emphasizing salvation only after the believer endures "to the last day" (*Mosiah 26:23*).

This is spiritual suicide and contrasts sharply with the Gospel. Biblically, peace is not withheld until after human effort. God gives peace now, in our weakness, not as a reward for spiritual performance, but as a result of Christ's finished work. "We put no confidence in human effort" (Phil. 3:3, NLT); "My grace is all you need. My power works best in weakness" (2 Corinthians 12:9 NLT).

PRIDE

CHRISTIANITY

In Biblical Scripture, pride is the belief that success or security comes from ourselves rather than God's grace.

1 John 2:16 NIV "For everything in the world–the lust of the flesh, the lust of the eyes, and the pride of life–comes not from the Father but from the world."

The biblical pattern is clear:

1. Obedience to God brings blessings, peace, and prosperity. (Deuteronomy 28:1-14).
2. Self-sufficiency grows, and people forget their dependence on God. (Deuteronomy 8:10-17; Hosea 13:6).
3. Pride leads to sin, greed, injustice, idolatry, and loss of blessing. (Isaiah 5:21-23).
4. Through suffering or conviction, people repent and turn back to God. (Deuteronomy 8:2-5; 2 Chronicles 7:14).
5. God, in mercy, forgives and restores. (Isaiah 1:18).

Example: Jonah ignored God's command to warn Nineveh. God sent a storm, <u>not to destroy</u> Jonah, but to redirect him. After repentance, Nineveh turned to God and was spared (Jonah 1–4). In Christianity, God humbles to save, not to shame.

MORMONISM

The Book of Mormon describes a similar pride cycle, but often tied to human effort and outward material prosperity:

1. *Human Humility* brings blessings and wealth. *(Helaman 12:1-3)*
2. Material prosperity leads to pride and forgetting God. *(Helaman 13:20-22)*
3. Pride produces sin, often *linked* to love of money, and calamity follows. *(Helaman 13:22-23)*
4. <u>Suffering</u> forces repentance (often fear-based) *(Helaman 12:3; Alma 32:13-14)*.
5. God restores prosperity, and the cycle repeats. *(Alma 62:48; Helaman 5:12-13)*.

Mormon scripture verses such as *Ether 12:27* and *2 Nephi 25:23* show a grace-after-effort model: *"...for we know that it is by grace we are saved, <u>after all we can do</u>."* This can foster pride in humility, where it is based on human effort.

In *Mormon* culture, circumstances are often seen as God's judgment, blessing for good choices, hardship for bad. But the BIBLICAL God gives peace <u>in the midst of storms,</u> not just after they pass.

BREATH

I am forever grateful to the God who keeps me breathing. Every breath you take is gifted air from His goodness. He doesn't promise us tomorrow. The very breath in our lungs is His gift.

Job declares this plainly: "For the Spirit of God has made me, and the breath of the Almighty gives me life" (Job 33:4, NLT). Scripture teaches that our breath is not random, it is intentional, personal, and sustained by God Himself.

The Hebrew language gives rich insight into this truth.

- napah (נָפַח) – "to blow," the act of breathing
- neshamah/nsama (נְשָׁמָה) – "breath," the life-breath inside a person
- ruach/ruah (רוּחַ) – "spirit, wind, breath," often referring to the Spirit of God

God blew (napah) into Adam's nostrils the breath (neshamah) of life (Gen 2:7, NLT). When the widow's son died, Scripture says, "there was no breath left in him" (neshamah, 1 Kings 17:17, NLT). And the Spirit of God, the ruah, is the divine breath that moved over the waters at creation (Gen 1:2).

In simple terms, God "bent down" and breathed life into humanity. His breath (neshamah) filled Adam's lungs, and His Spirit (ruah) remained with him to guide,

"

comfort, and sustain. That means every inhale is God's mercy, and every exhale is grace.

The Bible consistently presents breath as a gift, freely given by a loving Creator who sustains our life moment by moment.

MORMONISM

When we examine how *Mormon* scripture speaks of breath, a very different picture appears. The *Book of Mormon* uses the term "breath" about **six times**, an enormous contrast with the Bible's rich and frequent use of **55+ times**.

In *Mormon Mosiah 2*, breath is not portrayed as a loving gift but as something "lent", implying temporary ownership, indebtedness, and obligation:

- *"He is preserving you from day to day, by lending you breath, that ye may live and move and do according to your own will" (Mosiah 2:21).*
- *"...ye are even less than the dust of the earth" (Mosiah 2:25).*

The theological message is clear: the *Mormon* god grants breath as a loan, and humanity exists in constant debt—morally, spiritually, and functionally. Instead of breath being a gift from a loving Father, it becomes evidence that the individual owes God payment through obedience, endurance, and worthiness.

Where Scripture presents God as the One who lovingly breathes life into His children and sustains them with His Spirit, Mormon doctrine reframes that breath as conditional and transactional. The biblical God is generous; the Mormon god is exacting. The Bible offers dignity; Mormon scripture diminishes man to "less than the dust."

The contrast is unmistakable:

The God of the Bible gives breath freely.

The god of Mormonism lends breath conditionally.

ARK OF THE COVENANT VS GOLDEN PLATES

CHRISTIANITY

In the following scriptures, we learn about the Biblical <u>Ark of the Covenant</u> (get ready, its long winded): (Exodus 25:10-22; Exodus 37:1-9; Numbers 10:33-36; Joshua 3-4; Samuel 4-7; 2 Samuel 6; 1 Kings 8; Hebrews 9:4). We learn of <u>The contents</u> of the Ark in Hebrews 9:4, that it contained two stone tablets of the Ten Commandments, Aaron's rod that budded, and a golden pot of Manna. The ark was made of acacia wood, overlaid with pure gold with two gold cherubim (angels) on the lid called the Mercy Seat. There were rings and poles for carrying, never to be touched directly. The spiritual and symbolic meaning of the Ark was that it contained God's presence, God's throne on earth in the Old Testament, where he would speak with Moses (Exodus 25:22), and it held the testimony of the covenant between God and Israel. On the Day of Atonement, the high priest sprinkled blood on the Mercy Seat (Leviticus 16), symbolizing God's forgiveness. The Ark parted rivers (Joshua 3), brought victory or judgments in battle, and caused plagues when misused (1 Samuel 5-6). The ark was built at Mount Sinai (Exodus 25-40), carried through the wilderness, parted the Jordan River for the Israelites (Joshua 3), brought down Jericho's walls (Joshua 6), captured by Philistines, caused plagues (1 Samuel 4-6), returned to

Israel, and stayed at Kiriath-Jearim for 20 years (1 Samuel 7:1-2). King David moves it to Jerusalem (2 Samuel 6), places the ark in Solomon's Temple (1 Kings 8), and then the ark disappears from history, meaning it is not mentioned after the Babylonian conquest in 586 BC.

The biblical symbolism is amazing. The ark pointed to Jesus Christ as the fulfillment of God's covenant. The Mercy seat is now Christ's atonement. The Law inside the Ark is fulfilled by Christ. The Manna is Jesus, the bread of life (John 6:35), and Aaron's Rod is Christ's resurrection power.

MORMONISM

However, *Mormon* founder *Joseph Smith* speaks of golden plates and brings many similarities and elements from the ark of the covenant. It's important to remember that *Joseph Smith* had the Bible from a young age and was aware of its stories and themes.

Joseph Smith claimed in the early 1800s to have discovered golden plates buried in the *Hill Cumorah* (no archaeological evidence for this hill), guided by an angel named *Moroni*. He later said he translated them into the Book of Mormon using a seer stone placed in a hat, a method never modeled or endorsed in Scripture, but used for criminal activity in this day called "Treasure Digging". *Smith* also claimed that people would be struck dead if they tried to view or touch the plates unworthily, paralleling biblical stories like that of the Ark, yet without any divine command or biblical precedent. It is important to note that *Smith* says he used the Urim and Thummim in 1827 to also help him translate the Book of Mormon, he says these two stones helped him dictate English words from "Reformed Egyptian".

His attempt to establish new scripture and set himself up as a prophet like Moses contradicts Jesus' own promise that His church would not fall:

"On this rock I will build my church, and the gates of Hades will not overcome it." – Matthew 16:18

There was no need for a "restoration" of the gospel. Christ's victory is complete, and His Word is sufficient.

BAPTISM

In the Bible, John the Baptist gave a baptism of repentance and spoke of a man greater than himself who would bring the fire of the Holy Spirit to believers:

Matthew 3:11 NLT, "I baptize with water those who repent of their sins and turn to God. But someone is coming soon who is greater than I am, so much greater that I'm not worthy even to be his slave and carry his sandals. He will baptize you with the Holy Spirit and with fire."

Let's break this verse down a bit:

John makes it clear that his baptism with water is only a baptism of repentance, a preparation. He points forward to Christ, who alone brings the baptism that truly saves: the baptism of the Holy Spirit and fire.

In this next passage, we see that water baptism is not an ordinance of salvation at all, but a signpost leading to Christ:

Acts 19:1–6, Paul encounters believers who had only received John's baptism. He explains that John's baptism pointed them to believe in Jesus. Once they heard this, they were baptized in the name of the Lord Jesus, and then received the Holy Spirit.

We also learn that preaching the Good News is superior to baptizing with water:

1 Corinthians 1:14–18, Paul even thanks God that he baptized very few people, because his mission was not to baptize but to preach Christ crucified. The power of salvation is not found in the water, but in the cross of Christ.

And the ultimate example? The thief on the cross. He was never baptized with water, yet Jesus Himself promised him eternal life:

Luke 23:42–43, "Then he said, 'Jesus, remember me when you come into your Kingdom.' And Jesus replied, 'I assure you, today you will be with me in paradise.'"

MORMONISM

In the *Mormon church*, however, baptism with water is considered a <u>saving ordinance</u>. Because of this belief, they even practice baptism for the dead, where living members are baptized on behalf of those who have already passed away, so everyone is given a supposed chance to accept Mormonism (see more in Chapter: Baptisms For The Dead).

Here is Mormon scripture:

2 Nephi 31:5, "And now, if the Lamb of God, he being holy, should have need to be baptized by water, to fulfil all righteousness, O then, how much more need have we, being unholy, to be baptized, yea, even by water!"

(Mormons are missing the whole point here. If all Jesus ever needed to do was dip Himself in water, then we could all be called "god" for dipping ourselves in water! The difference between Jesus and us is that He was never in sin. He is perfect. Jesus is God..)

1 John 3:5 ASV "And ye know that he was manifested to take away sins; and in him is <u>no</u> sin."

2 Corinthians 5:21, "For he hath made him to be sin for us, who knew no sin; that we might be made the righteousness of God in him."

Colossians 2:9, "For in him dwelleth all the fulness of the Godhead bodily."

Mormons also recite the Fourth Article of Faith weekly:

"We believe that the first principles and ordinances of the Gospel are: first, Faith in the Lord Jesus Christ; second, Repentance; third, Baptism by immersion for the remission of sins; fourth, Laying on of hands for the gift of the Holy Ghost."

Notice this phrase: *"for the remission of sins."*

The reason they are baptizing is FOR the REMISSION of sins. That rhetoric totally replaces Jesus Christ with the ordinance. You have now become your own savior.

But the Bible says Jesus Himself paid for your sins:

John 3:16, "For God so loved the world, that he gave his only begotten Son, that whosoever believeth in him should not perish, but have everlasting life."

Mormons will also use John 3:5 to support their teaching:

John 3:5 NLT, "Jesus replied, 'I assure you, no one can enter the Kingdom of God without being born of water and the Spirit.'"

But biblically, Jesus is telling Nicodemus that "born of water" means natural birth, as the very next verse clarifies:

John 3:6 KJV, "That which is born of the flesh (water) is flesh; and that which is born of the Spirit is spirit."

We are all born of the flesh once, but we must be born again by the Spirit.

WORKS

Law gives notice of what sin actually is (Romans 3:20), but we were never meant to be able to follow all the rules as mere humans. Galatians 5:18 NLT "But when you are directed by the Spirit, you are not under obligation to the law of Moses."

Romans 6:15 NLT "Well, then, since God's grace has set us free from the law, does that mean we can go on sinning? Of course not!"

Good works don't earn salvation, but they flow out of salvation (already saved). Christians are called to Love God and Love others (Matthew 22:37-39), live holy lives (1 Peter 1:15-16), practice forgiveness, generosity, kindness (Colossians 3:12-14), and share the gospel (Matthew 28:19-20).

These aren't a checklist to gain heaven, they are evidence that someone already belongs to Christ. Jesus said these words when he spoke of the laws of Moses's time: Matthew 5:17-18 "Think not that I am come to destroy the law, or the prophets: I am not come to destroy, but to fulfill." Yes, He is a gift. Yes, he did it for you. Yes, you can have hope in him. Yes, he saved you from all the wreckage.

MORMONISM

Mormons live by works and believe living worthily gets them entrance into Heaven, <u>earning</u> salvation. That is

why they are so nice. You will never meet a mean
Mormon. There are over six thousand rules, but I will list
20 main ones that are in addition to the Ten
Commandments that were brought by a man named Joseph
Smith + other leaders of the LDS church:

1. *Read the Book of Mormon as superior to
    the Bible. Study the Book of Mormon,
    Doctrine and Covenants (D&C), and Pearl
    of Great Price, then the Bible. Review
    Ensign and New Era monthly LDS church
    magazines.*
2. *Participate in General Conference, listen to
    30+ men of the church (3-5 women) speak
    for 10 hours in one weekend every 6
    months.*
3. *Repent and turn away from mormon sin:
    sexual sin, immodest clothing, coffee
    drinking, tea drinking, alcohol, dishonesty,
    tattoos, stealing. Confessing mormon sins
    to God and in some cases to a leader in the
    bishopric.*
4. *Participate in the saving Ordinance of
    Baptism by Immersion for the remission of
    sins in water at age 8, and receive the holy
    ghost by confirmation with the laying on of
    hands on your head (very physical, not
    spiritual).*
5. *Pay a consistent full tithe of 10% and give
    fast offerings once a month, annual
    interviews to make sure this is consistent.*
6. *Be worthy to enter the temple with a temple
    recommend, by answering interview
    questions correctly, having no dealings with
    those opposed to your mormon faith.*
7. *Wear garments (mormon underwear) daily.
    Only taken off for s**, swim, and exercise.*

8. *Go to Church and partake in weekly sacrament (bread + water) to wash away sins weekly, as well as participate in church duties, responsibilities, and callings.*

9. *Fast the first Sunday of every month and give the money you would have paid for a meal for your family to fast offering (example family of 5 = $75 fast offering given).*

10. *Temple Worship: participate in ordinances and covenants in the temple like baptism for the dead, marriage sealing for the dead, and endowment ceremonies + participate in family history work.*

11. *Missionary work, men at the age of eighteen are <u>required</u> to go on a 2-year Mormon mission. Women are encouraged at age nineteen to go if they are not already married since their first priority is birthing children (more members).*

12. *Following the Word of Wisdom—adhering to the health code from D&C 89: abstaining from alcohol, tobacco, high energy drinks, coffee, and tea, eating meats sparingly.*

13. *Chastity and Sexual Purity—living a life of chastity before marriage and fidelity within marriage. Premarital sexual relations and any form of sexual immorality (such as pornography) are considered sinful.*

14. *Living a Moral Life—Avoiding lying, cheating, gambling, stealing, or engaging in other unethical behaviors. Volunteer your service and time to the needy and the elderly, be kind, be good citizens and observe the law of the land.*

15. *Keeping a clean exterior: One set of piercings, only one on each ear. No tattoos whatsoever. No showing of belly, shoulders (before year 2025), upper thigh or back.*
16. *Observing the Sabbath Day: going to church and resting, members are told to avoid shopping, unnecessary labor, or recreational activities that do not bring them closer to God on Sundays.*
17. *Accepting Church Counsel: Following the counsel and guidance of church leaders as you would scripture. Members are expected to listen to and follow the teachings and advice of church leaders, particularly as it pertains to spiritual and doctrinal matters.*
18. *Avoiding Pornography and Immorality: Staying away from pornography, immoral content, and other inappropriate behavior and are encouraged to keep their thoughts and actions pure.*
19. *Sustaining Church Leaders: Supporting and sustaining the leaders of the church by the raising of the right hand. Members are encouraged to pray for their leaders, follow their counsel, and support the church's initiatives.*
20. *Teach your children Mormonism: said to be the MOST IMPORTANT WORK (legacy obviously).*

What happens when we take rules away? What happens when we are no longer governed by man? What happens when you observe Jesus's rules only? Love the Lord your God with all your heart, and second, love others as yourself?

A SAVIOR SAVES

CHRISTIANITY

The literal definition of a savior without religion is "a person who rescues another from danger." If we don't realize the danger we were in, we wouldn't understand that we are sinners headed for destruction–hellfilre and brimstone. Without that awareness, we won't see our need for a supernatural Savior who is altogether outside of us. Heaven forbid we must hit rock bottom before we look up–yet it's often in that place of utter brokenness that many of us finally find Him. Also, if you don't understand your enemy, you won't understand what the Savior also gave you authority over. So who is he?

1 Peter 5:8 "Be sober-minded; be watchful. Your adversary the devil prowls around like a roaring lion, seeking someone to devour."

John 10:10 "The thief comes only to steal and kill and destroy. I came that they may have life and have it abundantly."

As Believers in Jesus, we have power over the enemy because God put the enemy under his feet and we are God's CHILDREN. He has given us authority to tread on serpents (Luke 10:19).

The Word is clear what our God saved us from:
- Hebrews 9:22: Without the shedding of blood, there is no forgiveness of sins.
- Leviticus 17:11: Blood is required to atone for souls on the altar.
- Hebrews 10:18: The blood of Christ's body was poured out <u>for the forgiveness of sins.</u>

- Romans 3:25: God provided Jesus as the atoning sacrifice to demonstrate His righteousness.
- Ephesians 1:7: Jesus Christ is the one through whom redemption and forgiveness are made possible.

MORMONISM

Mormons believe that Jesus' atonement automatically covers children from birth until age 8. After baptism at age 8, however, they teach that forgiveness of sins is no longer automatic. Instead, members must go through a six-step repentance process, and for serious sins they must confess to their bishop. They believe Christ's atonement is applied to each sin as it is repented of, and that His grace will cover any sins forgotten or overlooked. In their view, children who die before age 8 are considered sinless and go directly to God's kingdom, which can be seen as a form of child idealization. They also believe that those who never heard the Mormon gospel in this life, for example, someone in a remote place, will also enter God's kingdom.

Mormons use the term *savior* but are not speaking of the Savior who saved them. They believe in the word *atonement*, but they believe half of this was accomplished in the Garden of Gethsemane, where he sweat (*bled*) from every pore. Doctrinally, this could pose an issue between God willingly sweating or God willingly being beaten to death and murdered (nobody takes his life he lays it down).

If we are not believers in the one who saved us, the Word says this:

John 8:44 "You are of your father the devil, and your will is to do your father's desires. He was a murderer from the beginning, and has nothing to do with the truth, because there is no truth in him. When he lies, he speaks out of his own character, for he is a liar and the father of lies."

Mormon god, their "savior" threatens his people with scripture D&C 19:15-19, *15 Therefore I command you to repent, repent, lest I smite you by the rod of my mouth, and by my wrath, and by my anger, and your sufferings be sore, how sore you know not, how exquisite you know not, yea, how hard to bear you know not. 16 For behold, I, God, have suffered these things for all, that they might not suffer if they would repent; 17 But if they would not repent they must suffer even as I; 18 Which suffering caused myself, even God, the greatest of all, to tremble because of pain, and to bleed at every pore, and to suffer both body and spirit, and would that I might not drink the bitter cup, and shrink 19 Nevertheless, glory be to the Father, and I partook and finished my preparations unto the children of men.*

Their god sounds like a bully. He sounds like an unwilling and threatening god. He seems like a victim here. He does not exemplify the biblical God in any capacity!

You will hear most Mormons use phrases like "I love my Savior," "I know my Savior loves me," and "I know my Savior lives." But they are just afraid of their mormon god. They use the phrase "tender mercies" way too often and are not speaking of the biblical Savior who FINISHED THE WORK (John 19:30 "...tetelestai..").

Before I move on, if you are a Mormon and you would like to be saved TODAY into the Heavenly Kingdom where Jesus sits currently on the right hand of the Father, say these words OUT LOUD and believe in your heart: "Lord God, I know I am a SINNER in need of forgiveness. Thank you for dying FOR ME on the cross of Calvary two thousand years ago and finishing the work for salvation. YOU SHED YOUR BLOOD FOR ME! YOU SAID IT IS FINISHED! I believe in you, Jesus, and I thank you for forgiving me of ALL MY sin. I invite you into my heart to heal me, to stir me, to encourage me, and to love me the way that only you can. I say this in your name, JESUS, AMEN."

If you said that prayer, please locate a Christian church near you and tell them you've been SAVED. They'll take it from there. You will never be the same again! Welcome into CHRIST'S BODY!

THE BIBLE and JOSEPH'S CHANGES TO IT

CHRISTIANITY

We know the Bible is to remain unchanged, as the Bible itself says: 2 Timothy 3:16 "All scripture is given by inspiration of God, and is profitable for doctrine, for reproof, for correction, for instruction in righteousness."

The Bible also states that nothing will be strong enough to defeat the church, not even hell: Matthew 16:18 NLT "Now I say to you that you are Peter [which means 'rock'], and upon this rock I will build my church, and all the powers of hell will not conquer it."

MORMONISM

While JESUS clearly states that the gates of Hades will not prevail against the church, *Joseph Smith* taught his followers that the Bible words were lost, removed, and distorted. He also taught that the Bible word was not fully preserved and is incomplete, lacking fullness and plain and precious truths. Joseph Smith reiterated his narrative by adding to the original Bible verses as in the examples below: (I will place the original Bible verse first and *Joseph Smith's translation italicized* second)

1. "Woe unto you, lawyers! for ye have taken away the key of knowledge: ye entered not in yourselves, and them that were entering in ye hindered." (Luke 11:52 KJV)

2. *"Woe unto you, lawyers! for ye have taken away the key of knowledge, <u>the fullness of the scriptures</u>"* (Luke 11:52 **Joseph Smith Translation** JST)

In this instance, Joseph Smith drew on a biblical scripture but altered its meaning, presenting it in a way that framed the coming Book of Mormon as 'the fullness of scripture.'

In the Bible in Luke 11:52, Jesus is actually calling out the scribes and Pharisees as hypocrites. They claim to be wise and knowledgeable, but they don't enter the knowledge themselves, and instead, they prevent others from entering. Jesus is addressing the <u>behavior</u> of the religious leaders, not the scriptures themselves. He is not implying anything about the teachings of *Joseph Smith* or any other scriptures beyond the Bible.

Here is another example of Joseph making changes to the Bible itself:

1. "If I bear witness of myself, my witness **is not** true." (John 5:31 **KJV**)

2. *"Therefore if I bear witness of myself, yet my witness <u>is</u> true."* (John 5:32 **Joseph Smith Translation** [JST])

In this change, Joseph completely changes the words of God. It is important to note his changes to the Bible aren't minor adjustments. In many cases, these changes completely alter the meaning of the verses, and in some instances, they even reverse the original meaning as in the example just provided.

For the sake of this book's page count, I will provide only 20 more examples, though there are many more, of where Joseph Smith altered biblical verses to fit <u>his own</u> narrative. In each case, I will place the original

Bible verse first (KJV), followed by Joseph Smith's changes (JST) in *italics*:

"God is spirit." **(John 4:24 KJV)**
"For unto such hath God promised his spirit." **(John 4:26 JST)**

"For they shall be filled." **(Matthew 5:6 KJV)**
"For they shall be filled with the Holy Ghost." **(Matthew 5:8 JST)**

"Ye are the salt of the earth." **(Matthew 5:13 KJV)**
"I give unto you to be the salt of the earth." **(Matthew 5:15 JST)**

"Ye are the light of the world." **(Matthew 5:14 KJV)**
"I give unto you to be the light of the world." **(Matthew 5:16 JST)**

"And no man receiveth his testimony." **(John 3:32 KJV)**
"And but few men receive his testimony." **(John 3:32 JST)**

"When Jesus heard it, he marvelled, and said to them that followed." **(Matthew 8:10 KJV)**
"And when they that followed him, heard this, they marvelled." **(Matthew 8:9 JST)**

"Be ye therefore wise as serpents." **(Matthew 10:16 KJV)**
"Be ye therefore wise servants." **(Matthew 10:14 JST)**

"Teaching for doctrines the commandments of men." **(Matthew 15:9 KJV)**
"Teaching the doctrines and the commandments of men." **(Matthew 15:8 JST)**

"As touching any thing that they shall ask, it shall be done for them." **(Matthew 18:19 KJV)**

"As touching any thing that they shall ask, that they may not ask amiss, it shall be done for them." **(Matthew 18:19 JST)**

"Verily I say unto you, I know you not." **(Matthew 25:12 KJV)**
"Verily I say unto you, Ye know me not." **(Matthew 25:11 JST)**

"And were all baptized of him." **(Mark 1:5 KJV)**
"And many were baptized of him." **(Mark 1:4 JST)**

"Except they wash, they eat not." **(Mark 7:4 KJV)**
"Except they wash their bodies, they eat not." **(Mark 7:4 JST)**

"There shall no sign be given unto this generation."
(Mark 8:12 KJV)
"There shall no sign be given unto this generation, save the sign of the prophet Jonah." **(Mark 8:12 JST)**
"Passed by on the other side." **(Luke 10:32 KJV)**
"Passed by on the other side of the way; for they desired in their hearts that it might not be known that they had seen him." **(Luke 10:33 JST)**

"We have done that which was our duty to do." **(Luke 17:10 KJV)**
"We have done that which was no more than our duty to do." **(Luke 17:10 JST)**

"And ye shall be hated of all men for my name's sake."
(Luke 21:17 KJV)
"And ye shall be hated of all the world for my name's sake." **(Luke 21:16 JST)**

"That he may sift you as wheat." **(Luke 22:31 KJV)**
"That he may sift the children of the kingdom as wheat." **(Luke 22:31 JST)**

"Which the Son of man shall give unto you." **(John 6:27 KJV)**
"Which the Son of Man hath power to give unto you." **(John 6:27 JST)**

"Neither do I condemn thee: go, and sin no more." **(John 8:11 KJV)**
"Neither do I condemn thee: go, and sin no more. And the woman glorified God from that hour, and believed on his name." **(John 8:11 JST)**

"Ye did not hear: wherefore would ye hear it again?" **(John 9:27 KJV)**
"Ye did not believe: wherefore would you believe if I should tell you again?" **(John 9:27 JST)**

These alterations shift the focus away from Christ as the eternal Savior, instead teaching that individuals can achieve salvation through their own works. This creates the false idea that salvation is earned through personal effort, rather than being a gift from Jesus Christ, which is contrary to the true Gospel message.

ONE MORE THOUGHT:

Mormons will criticize Christians for having so many Bible translations, but these are paraphrased changes, for example, the New Living Translation and the King James Version:

"For this is how God loved the world: He gave his one and only Son, so that everyone who believes in him will not perish but have eternal life." **(NLT)**

"For God so loved the world, that he gave his only begotten Son, that whosoever believeth in him should not perish, but have everlasting life." **(KJV)**

While some words may differ, the meaning and context of the verses remain unchanged and have not been distorted in any way!

Are you still with me? Another example of a biblical translation that does not change the meaning of the verses is John 1:1. Across four different Bible translations, the translations remain faithful to the original message without altering its meaning:

John 1:1 "In the beginning the Word already existed. The Word was with God, and the Word was God." **(NLT)**
John 1:1 "In the beginning was the Word, and the Word was with God, and the Word was God." **(KJV)**
John 1:1 "In the beginning was the Word, and the Word was with God, and the Word was God." **(New American Standard Bible)**
John 1:1 "In the beginning [before all time] was the Word [Christ], and the Word was with God, and the Word was God Himself" **(Amplified Bible [AB]).**

However, Joseph Smith's changes are much more significant, altering the core meaning of the verses themselves:

Mormon John 1:1 "In the beginning was the *gospel preached through the Son. And the gospel was the Word,* and the *Word* was with *the son, and the son was with God,* and the *Son was of* God." **(JST)**

There are now 16+ million members of the Mormon church who believe in this foolishness.

Being that the KJV Bible is highly accurate in translation, Joseph should have **<u>no need</u>** to make these significant changes to it.

TITHING

God loves a CHEERFUL GIVER. If you're feeling obligated or compelled to give, don't! Please don't! Cain gave a similar offering in Genesis 4.

2 Corinthians 9:7 "Each of you should give what you have decided in your heart to give, not reluctantly or under compulsion, for God loves a cheerful giver."

God doesn't need your money; He owns everything. What He desires is your heart, which is why this verse focuses on your heart, not the amount. A perfect example of this is Jesus's parable of the widow with two mites, according to which her heart and sacrifice mattered more than the value of her offering (Mark 12:42).

The tithe was originally part of Israel's covenant law, tied to the Temple, the Levites, and the land of Israel. A few examples are: Abram gave Melchizedek a tenth of everything (Genesis 14:20), Jacob vowed to give God a tenth (Genesis 28:22), a tithe supported the Levites (Numbers 18:21), and tithe was used for worship, celebration and helping the poor (Deuteronomy 14:22).

The Lord tells his followers to test him and "see if I will not throw open the floodgates of heaven, and pour you out a blessing, that there shall not be room enough to receive it" (Malachi 3:10). Christians are not commanded in this capacity, legally bound as Christ fulfilled the law. We are to give freely, generously, and cheerfully. God's blessing to "rebuke the devourer on our behalf" is no longer tied to tithing, but to grace and faith in Christ. However, many Christians see giving generously (whether 10% or more) as a way to honor God first, and many

Pastors use the 10% tithe as a good rule of thumb or "baby step" to giving.

2 Corinthians 9:6 NLT "Remember this–a farmer who plants only a few seeds will get a small crop. But the one who plants generously will get a generous crop."

MORMONISM

Mormons give 10% of their income as a rule to remain in good standing with the church. It is not from the heart, it is fixed. That 10% is **required** to have a Temple Recommend pass to get into each temple, which is taught to be the most important work a Mormon can do. During yearly interviews called tithing settlements, bishops ask members if they are "full-tithe payers." Only those who are may enter LDS temples, which are viewed as essential for exaltation (The Church of Jesus Christ of Latter-day Saints, n.d.-b).

Members are taught to give through the Church rather than directly to those in need. Each month, they make a fast offering, the value of two missed meals, by sealing the donation in an envelope and giving it to their bishop, who distributes funds to the needy (The Church of Jesus Christ of Latter-day Saints, n.d.-a; Doctrine and Covenants 107:68).

The *LDS* Church also profits from sales of temple garments, required clothing for endowed members—priced between $4 and $6 per piece, with temple outfits costing $80–$100 (Gillum, 2024; The Church of Jesus Christ of Latter-day Saints, n.d.-c). These are worn daily as reminders of sacred covenants.

FINISHED

The biblical God has finished the work of salvation. Jesus said, "My food is to do the will of Him who sent Me and to finish His work" (John 4:34). On the cross, "Jesus, knowing that everything had now been accomplished, said, 'I am thirsty'" (John 19:28). Then He declared, "It is finished" (Tetelestai), and gave up His spirit (John 19:30). Earlier, He prayed, "I have finished the work which You gave Me to do" (John 17:4).

The Greek word Tetelestai (from teleō) means to finish, complete, accomplish, or pay in full. In the ancient world, servants or debtors used it to announce that a task or payment was fully completed. Jesus used it to proclaim that the debt of sin was paid in full, nothing more can be added. As He said, "I came not to abolish the Law or the Prophets but to accomplish their purpose" (Matthew 5:17). Through His death and resurrection, God completed redemption "once for all" (Hebrews 10:10).

Faith comes not from works but from hearing the Good News: "Faith comes by hearing, and hearing through the word of Christ" (Romans 10:17). "The gospel… is the power of God unto salvation" (Romans 1:16). Scripture warns against adding to this finished gospel: "Even if we or an angel from heaven should preach another gospel… let him be accursed" (Galatians 1:8).

MORMONISM

The *Mormons* believe that God's work is ongoing, and that He continues to reveal additional scripture beyond the Bible. According to their own writings, those who claim the Bible alone is complete and canonized are considered foolish: *2 Nephi 29:6 Thou fool, that shall say: A ⁿBible, we have got a Bible, and we need no more Bible..."*

2nd Nephi goes on to criticize Christians: *"...Have ye obtained a Bible save it were by the Jews? 7 Know ye not that there are more ⁿnations than one? Know ye not that I, the Lord your God, have created all men, and that I remember those who are upon the ᵇisles of the sea; and that I rule in the heavens above and in the ᶜearth beneath; and I bring forth my ᵈword unto the children of men, yea, even upon all the nations of the earth? 8 Wherefore murmur ye, because that ye shall receive more of my word? Know ye not that the ⁿtestimony of ᵇtwo nations is a ᶜwitness unto you that I am God, that I remember one ᵈnation like unto another?..."*

The devil, the manipulator continues: *"...Wherefore, I speak the same words unto one nation like unto another. And when the two ᵉnations shall run together the testimony of the two nations shall run together also. 9 And I do this that I may prove unto many that I am the ⁿsame yesterday, today, and forever; and that I speak forth my ᵇwords according to mine own pleasure. <u>And because that I have spoken one ᶜword ye need not suppose that I cannot speak another; for my ᵈwork is not yet finished;</u> neither shall it be until the end of man, neither from that time henceforth and <u>forever</u>.*

In *Mormon* teaching, their god claims that his work is NEVER FINISHED! Such an opposing teaching to Christianity. He speaks in a condemning tone, giving himself permission to add to the Bible. Rather than granting true freedom as the Bible canonized holds, he controls and pressures his followers, treating them more like slaves than children who are free in Christ. He has placed them back into that same Old Testament mindset of bondage, convincing them that Jesus's work was not finished on the cross, and is never finished, in order to keep them enslaved and under his control.

I'll conclude this chapter with a simple bible verse: 1 Corinthians 1:18 NIV, "for the message of the cross is foolishness to those who are perishing, but to us who are being saved it is the power of God."

PROPHETS

Through the Bible we learn that 300+ prophecies come to pass from the Old Testament to new. Major prophets like: Isaiah, Jeremiah, Lamentations, Ezekiel, and Daniel. Minor prophets like: Hosea, Joel, Amos, Obadiah, Jonah, Micah, Nahum, Habakkuk, Zephaniah, Haggai, Zechariah, Malachi. There are also other prophetic people scattered throughout the Old Testament like: Moses, Samuel, Nathan, Elijah, and Elisha.

Some of these predictions we know well are as follows:

1. Born of a woman (Genesis 3:15, fulfilled in Matthew 2, Luke 2)
2. Born in Bethlehem (Micah 5:2, fulfilled Matthew 2, Luke 2)
3. Born of a virgin (Isaiah 7:14, fulfilled in Matthew 1, Luke 1)
4. Descendant of Abraham/Isaac/Jacob/David (Genesis + 2 Samuel, fulfilled in Matthew 1, Romans 1, Luke 3)
5. Preceded by a messenger (Isaiah 40:3, fulfilled in Matthew 3, Mark 1)
6. Enter Jerusalem on a donkey (Zechariah 9:9, fulfilled in Matthew 21, John 12)
7. Betrayed for thirty pieces of silver (Zechariah 11:12, fulfilled in Matthew 26-27)
8. Silent before accusers (Isaiah 53:7, fulfilled in Matthew 27, Mark 15)

9. Crucified/hands and feet pierced (Psalm 22 and Zechariah 12:10, fulfilled in John 19.
10. Resurrection (Psalm 16:10, fulfilled in Acts 2, Matthew 28, Luke 24)
11. Rejected by his own people (Isaiah 53:3, fulfilled in John 1, Luke 4)
12. Suffering servant/atoning suffering (Isaiah 53, fulfilled in 1 Peter 2)
13. A New Covenant (Jeremiah 31:31, fulfilled in Luke 22, Hebrews 8)
14. Outpouring of the Spirit (Joel 2:28, fulfilled in Acts 2)
15. Healing and miracles foretold (Isaiah 35 + 61, fulfilled in Luke 4)

We can conclude that these were real prophets based on the Bible scripture below:

Deuteronomy 18:22 NIV, "If what a prophet proclaims in the name of the Lord does not take place or come true, that is a message the Lord has not spoken. That prophet has spoken presumptuously, so do not be alarmed." The above listed prophecies have come true.

MORMONISM

Mormons believe that Joseph Smith was a prophet of God who was chosen to restore the true church on earth. In 1820, Joseph claimed that other churches were divided and full of contradictions, and that God called him to reestablish the one true church (Joseph Smith–History 1:19, Pearl of Great Price). By the standard of Deuteronomy 18:22, a true prophet's words must come to pass. Did any of Joseph Smith's prophecies actually come true? Let's take a look.

Smith declared that a temple would rise "in this generation" in Independence, Missouri in September 22-23,1832 (*D&C 84:2-5*), yet the site remains <u>vacant to this day</u>. He prophesied that apostle David Patten would go on a mission "next spring" in April 17, 1838 (*D&C 114*), but Patten was killed that October in the Battle of Crooked River and never served the mission. Smith even claimed that the Lord revealed Smith would live to age 85 (*D&C 130:14-17*), and if so, he would see Christ's return in 1835 (*History of the Church, volume 2, pg 182*). Smith died in 1844 at age 38, and Christ did not return by 1890. Each of these predictions failed the biblical test of prophecy.

Smith also inserted himself into scripture, reshaping Isaiah 29 in the Book of Mormon to portray himself as the "unlearned man" who would bring forth a sealed book:

For Comparison, I'll list Joseph Smith's words first,

Book of Mormon, 2 Nephi 27:12:

*"Wherefore, at that day when **the book** shall be **delivered unto the man** of **whom I have spoken**, the book shall be hid from the eyes of the world, that **the eyes of none** shall behold it save it be that **three witnesses** shall behold it, by the power of God, besides him to whom the book shall be delivered; and they shall testify to the truth of the book and the things therein*

v.15–17 "The book shall be delivered unto a man, and he shall deliver the words of the book… unto another… which shall say: I cannot bring the book, for it is sealed… Then shall the learned say: I cannot read it."

KJV Bible: Isaiah 29:11–12

v.11 "And the vision of all is become unto you as the words of a book that is sealed, which men deliver to one that is learned, saying, Read this, I pray thee: and he saith, I cannot; for it is sealed."

v.12 "And the book is delivered to him that is not learned, saying, Read this, I pray thee: and he saith, I am not learned."

In context, Isaiah 29 is a warning about spiritual blindness in Jerusalem, not a prediction about Joseph Smith or new scripture.

Even at the end of his life, Smith exalted himself: *"I have more to boast of than ever any man had ... Neither Paul, John, Peter, nor Jesus ever did it. I boast that no man ever did such a work as I" (History of the Church, 6:408–409).* Such words glorify man over God and stand in stark contrast to the humility of Christ and the prophets of Scripture.

Jesus promised that his church would never be destroyed (Matthew 16:18) and that his words would never pass away (Luke 21:33). If Christ's words endure, then there is no need for Smith's so-called restoration. By biblical standards, his failed prophecies confirm he was a false prophet.

BLOOD SACRIFICE

CHRISTIANITY

From the very beginning of mankind, the penalty for Adam's sin in taking the fruit was death-both physical and spiritual. Scripture shows us that the only way to overcome this penalty is through a blood sacrifice, a true atonement for sin:

OLD TESTAMENT: Leviticus 17:11 NIV, "For the life of a creature is in the blood, and I have given it to you to make atonement for yourselves on the altar; it is the blood that makes atonement for one's life."

NEW TESTAMENT: Hebrews 9:22 NIV, "In fact, the law requires that nearly everything be cleansed with blood, and without the shedding of blood there is no forgiveness."

Ephesians 1:7 NIV, "In him we have redemption through his blood, the forgiveness of sins, in accordance with the riches of God's grace."

One of the first examples of a blood sacrifice came directly from God Himself, when He provided animal skins to cover Adam and Eve after they sinned, showing that an innocent life had to be shed, foreshadowing what was to come. The Bible says clearly in Hebrews 10:12, that we "...have been made holy through the sacrifice of the body of Jesus Christ once for all."

Priests no longer have to visit the temple once a year to sacrifice the blood of goats and other animals, now the HIGH PRIEST (Hebrews 10:12) comes in one last time, ONCE FOR ALL, to atone for the blood of all mankind.

God does not need man for salvation; that is finished by the body of JESUS.

MORMONISM

Mormons believe that Christ's atoning blood sacrifice opened the way for salvation, but that individuals must ultimately achieve it themselves through obedience, keeping mormon commandments, and living morally:

"We believe that through the Atonement of Christ, all mankind may be saved, by obedience to the laws and ordinances of the Gospel." (Smith, J Articles of Faith, No. 3. In Pearl of Great Price. The Church of Jesus Christ of Latter-day Saints.)

Also, from LDS scripture, we learn that mormons are not saved by grace until "after all they can do":

2 Nephi 25:23 "....for we know that it is by grace that we are saved, after all we can do."

LET us be corrected with BIBLICAL SCRIPTURE: Colossians 2:20-23 ASV, "If ye died with Christ from the rudiments of the world, why, as though living in the world, do ye subject yourselves to ordinances, 21 Handle not, nor taste, nor touch 22 (all which things are to perish with the using), after the precepts and doctrines of men?

Ordinances are useless if you are a believer in Christ's atoning sacrifice. Jesus's blood is sufficient.

PROPHET'S VISIONS

CHRISTIANITY

The Old Testament prophets received visions and messages that pointed forward to Jesus Christ. Their prophecies were not random events but part of God's progressive revelation. Jesus affirms this when He says, "I did not come to abolish the law or the prophets … but to accomplish their purpose" (Matt 5:17, NLT). The Greek word for "fulfill" is plēroō, meaning to complete, bring to fullness (Blue Letter Bible, Strong's G4137).

Throughout Scripture, God revealed His plans through visions:

- Abraham received the covenant (Genesis 15; 17).
- Jacob saw the heavenly ladder (Genesis 28).
- Moses saw the burning bush (Exodus 3).
- Samuel received revelation about Eli's household (1 Samuel 3).
- Nathan prophesied David's dynasty (2 Samuel 7).
- Isaiah saw the Lord on His throne (Isaiah 6).
- Jeremiah saw the almond branch and boiling pot (Jeremiah 1).
- Ezekiel saw God's glory, the dry bones, and future temple (Ezekiel 1; 37; 40–48).
- Daniel saw kingdoms and the Ancient of Days (Daniel 7–12).

- The minor prophets, from Amos to Zechariah received visions of judgment, restoration, and the coming Messiah.

The New Testament continues this pattern. Joseph received visions about Jesus' birth (Matthew 1–2). Peter saw a sheet of unclean animals revealing God's plan for the Gentiles (Acts 10). Paul saw the risen Jesus and visions of guidance (Acts 9; 16; 2 Cor 12). And John received the Revelation, showing heaven, judgment, and new creation.

God affirms this prophetic method: "I, the Lord, reveal myself to them in visions; I speak to them in dreams" (Num 12:6, NLT).

But once Christ came, the prophetic office reached its fulfillment. Hebrews declares, "Long ago God spoke … through the prophets … but now in these final days, he has spoken to us through his Son" (Heb 1:1–2, NLT). Jesus Himself is the final, complete revelation.

Because Christ is now our Mediator, there is no longer a need for prophets in the Old Testament sense: "There is one God and one Mediator who can reconcile God and humanity, the man Christ Jesus" (1 Tim 2:5, NLT).

Some Christians believe the office of prophet has ended, while others believe the gift of prophecy, never equal with Scripture, continues because Peter quotes Joel saying we are living in the "last days" when visions and prophecy will appear among ordinary believers (Acts 2:16–18, NLT).

Acts records examples: Agabus predicting a famine (Acts 11), Philip's daughters who prophesied (Acts 21), and Paul's instructions to test prophecy carefully (1 Thess 5:20–21; 1 Cor 14:29).

The point is clear: the biblical pattern centers on Christ as the final revelation, and any prophetic activity after Him is subordinate to Scripture, not the foundation of new doctrine or new scripture.

MORMONISM

Mormonism teaches that there is one living prophet on earth at a time, beginning with Joseph Smith and continuing through a line of succession much like the papacy in Catholicism. Their prophetic line includes: Joseph Smith, Brigham Young, John Taylor, Wilford Woodruff, Lorenzo Snow, Joseph F. Smith, Heber J. Grant, George Albert Smith, David O. McKay, Joseph Fielding Smith, Harold B. Lee, Spencer W. Kimball, Ezra Taft Benson, Howard W. Hunter, Gordon B. Hinckley, Thomas S. Monson, Russell M. Nelson, and (by seniority) Dallin H. Oaks.

When one prophet dies, the longest-serving apostle becomes the next. This structure gives the LDS prophet authority to receive new revelations, change doctrine, alter practices, and reinterpret scripture.

Latter-day Saints are also instructed not to trust dreams or visions if they conflict with the church's leadership. The First Presidency stated:

"When visions, dreams, tongues, prophecy, impressions or any extraordinary gift or inspiration, convey something out of harmony with the accepted revelations of the Church or contrary to the decisions of its constituted authorities ... it is not of God."
(First Presidency, 1917, as cited by FAIR)

This places all personal revelation beneath institutional authority.

The foundational revelation of *Mormonism, Joseph Smith's The First Vision*, exists in multiple versions, varied deeply by the other, and acknowledged by LDS.org in their Gospel Topics Essay:

- 1832 account (Joseph's handwriting):
  One divine personage ("the Lord") forgives his sins. No mention of God the Father and Jesus as separate beings.
- 1835 accounts of the same divine encounter (diary entries):
  Describes two personages, similar in appearance, and "many angels."
- 1838 account of the same divine encounter (canonized as Joseph Smith—History):
  Two personages appear; The Father and The Son, one introduces the other as "My Beloved Son." This is the official version used today by Mormons.

The *Mormon LDS* Church teaches these differences are harmonious. Members accept these changes as part of "expanded understanding," just as they accept doctrinal and practical changes over time—including scripture revisions, policy reversals, and alterations to temple garments.

This contrasts sharply with the biblical pattern:

The prophets pointed to Christ.

Christ fulfilled the prophets,

and Scripture is complete.

THE APOSTASY

CHRISTIANITY

There is no known great apostasy in the Bible where the church disappeared. There were apostasies within groups or individuals, but not a worldwide, complete loss of the gospel. The Bible clearly affirms that Christ's Church would never be destroyed or removed from the earth. In Matthew 16:18, Jesus states, "Upon this rock I will build my church, and the gates of Hades shall not prevail against it," assuring its endurance throughout history. While Scripture does acknowledge apostasy, such as in 1 Timothy 4:1 and 2 Thessalonians 2:3, it presents it as a partial falling away, not a total disappearance. The gospel was "once for all delivered to the saints" (Jude 1:3), and God's Word declares in Ephesians 3:21 that there will be glory "in the church by Christ Jesus throughout all ages." The Holy Spirit, promised to remain with believers forever (John 14:16), guarantees the Church's ongoing life and truth. This is God's promise.

Isaiah 40:8 "The grass withers, the flower fades, but the word of our God will stand forever."

Matthew 24:35 "Heaven and earth will pass away, but my words will not pass away."

Early rulers tried to destroy the Bible, from King Jehoiakim (Jeremiah 36) to Roman Emperor Diocletian (AD 303), but every attempt failed. God preserved His word, through church fathers, and it remains the world's most widely read and translated book today.

MORMONISM

The Church of Jesus Christ of Latter-day Saints (Mormons) teach that after the deaths of Christ's apostles, a "Great Apostasy" occurred, a complete falling away from Christ's original Church and true doctrine and divine authority. They believe over time, human ideas and traditions replaced God's truth, leading to the development of Catholicism, Protestantism, and all other <u>Christian</u> denominations. As a result, Mormons believe that in the 1820s, God called Joseph Smith as a prophet to restore the true Church, which had been absent from the earth for over 1700 years. Joseph Smith claimed he saw God the Father and Jesus Christ (The "First Vision", which is ironic that it is actually the 3rd vision version recorded), who told him not to join any church and that all existing churches were corrupt. This restoration is said to have included new scripture (such as the Book of Mormon, Pearl of Great Price, Doctrine and Covenants), divine priesthood authority, and a reestablished church organization modeled after the early Christian church.

Also, according to *LDS teaching,* John the Baptist and later Peter, James, and John appeared to Joseph Smith to restore the Aaronic and Melchizedek priesthoods *(Joseph Smith-History 1:68-72; D&C 27:12-13; D&C 128:20).* BIBLICALLY, The Aaronic Priesthood was called "weak and useless" (Hebrews 7:18-19). Jesus Christ, our Eternal High Priest through the order of Melchizedek, has a perfect and unending priesthood-so there was no need for any restoration through man like Joseph Smith.)

(SIDE NOTE: The 400 years between the Old and New Testaments, a time without prophetic revelation, were foreordained and prophesied through Daniel's visions of future kingdoms (Daniel 2:31–45; 7:1–28) and God's message to Nebuchadnezzar (Daniel 2:36–44), which predicted the rise and fall of empires before the coming of Christ. Malachi, the final Old Testament prophet, also foretold this coming silence and waiting period, ending with the promise: "Look, I am sending you the prophet Elijah before the great and dreadful day of the Lord arrives" (Malachi 4:5, NLT). This silence was not spiritual loss but divine preparation, God orchestrating history to fulfill His promise of the Messiah at exactly the right time (Galatians 4:4, NLT). The Silence ended with John the Baptist's cry in the wilderness, approximately 1,778 years before Joseph Smith was ever born.)

The biblical record presents no need for a restoration through a modern prophet, because the Church has never ceased and God's truth has never been lost, as it had been carried through early church fathers.

THE TRINITY

CHRISTIANITY

The Bible teaches one God in three persons: God the Father, God the Son, and God the Holy Spirit, co-eternal, co-equal, and of one essence (John 1:1, John 10:30, John 14:23). God is Spirit (John 4:24), not confined to a body. The Nicene Creed affirms this: Jesus is "true God from true God… of the same essence as the Father," and the Spirit is worshiped with the Father and Son.

Though analogies like an egg or a three-leaf clover are sometimes used, they fall short, since no earthly example can capture the eternal Trinity. What Scripture makes clear is that God is one, yet three persons in perfect unity (Deut. 6:4; John 17:20–23). Jesus reveals God's power and identity through His Word: "Let there be light" (Gen. 1:3), "Lazarus, come forth" (John 11:43), and "I AM" (Exod. 3:14). Scripture continually affirms: "I am the LORD, and there is no other" (Isa. 45:5).

MORMONISM

Mormonism teaches three separate gods called the Godhead: Heavenly Father, Jesus, and the Holy Ghost, two with physical bodies (Heavenly Father and Jesus), one a spirit (Holy Spirit). In LDS teaching, Heavenly Father is supreme, Jesus is subordinate, and the Holy Ghost ranks third. Their temple films even portray Jesus as simply following orders from the Father.

This belief system:

1. Diminishes God by reducing Him to a being with a body.
2. Distorts the Trinity into polytheism—three gods instead of one.
3. Misidentifies the Spirit, treating Him as a separate deity and equating His leading with personal emotions (*"If it be right, you will feel a burning in your bosom; if it is not right, it will flee from you the thought"* (D&C 9:7–8).
4. Elevates humanity, teaching that people can become gods themselves. This gives false hope and elevates humankind to God's deity. It also stamps a multiple god monotheistic view.

In short, Mormonism departs from biblical monotheism and replaces the one true God with a hierarchy of deities and subjective feelings, directly contradicting the unity, spirit-nature, and supremacy of God revealed in Scripture.

THE WORD verses THE GOLDEN PLATES

CHRISTIANITY

The Bible stands as the Word of God, historically grounded and textually preserved. It has been copied with remarkable accuracy, over ninety-nine percent true to the original Hebrew and Greek manuscripts. Its truth is reinforced by archaeology and geography, for the people and places it names, Jerusalem, Bethlehem, Nazareth, Babylon, Egypt, are real locations that still stand today. The Scriptures testify directly of Christ: His birth, His miracles, His death, and His resurrection. These were not later inventions but eyewitness accounts of those who walked with Him. The Bible itself declares that the Word of God is living and indestructible, sharper than any two-edged sword (Hebrews 4:12), enduring forever (Isaiah 40:8). Nowhere in its pages does God ever say His church must be restored by another man or with another book. He Himself promises that the gates of hell will not prevail against His church (Matthew 16:18).

MORMONISM

In stark contrast, the *Book of Mormon* claims to be "another testament" of Jesus Christ, translated by Joseph Smith with a hat and a seer stone off from golden plates. The LDS church teaches that the plates were written in Reformed Egyptian (Mormon 9:32), though the language itself is not recognized by any historian or linguist.

Central to its story is a battle at the Hill Cumorah in which more than two hundred thousand people were killed, yet there is no archaeological evidence of such an event, no weapons, no armor, no remains. Beyond this, many of the book's names and themes can be traced not to the ancient world but to the early nineteenth century. The name "Moroni," for example, appears in tales of Captain Kidd's adventures near the Comoros Islands, stories widely known in Joseph Smith's day. Scholars have shown that Smith borrowed not only from such literature "but also from the King James Bible, the Apocrypha, Protestant revival preaching, American antiquities, and even Masonic ideas, weaving them together into his own narrative" (Runnels, 2017).

The Bible is anchored in verifiable history, eyewitness testimony, and the unchanging promises of God. The Book of Mormon, by contrast, lacks historical evidence and is built upon sources and ideas circulating in Joseph Smith's lifetime. Where Scripture reveals the eternal, sovereign Word of God, Mormonism substitutes a man-made story, claiming divine authority it does not possess.

STICK OF JUDAH, STICK OF JOSEPH

CHRISTIANITY

Ezekiel's vision of the two sticks reveals God's promise to reunite the divided kingdoms of Israel and Judah. The "stick of Judah" and the "stick of Joseph" symbolize two nations becoming one under a single king: "I will make them one nation…with one king to rule them all" (Ezekiel 37:22, NLT). Ephraim, often used to represent the Northern Kingdom, clarifies that the imagery refers to people groups, not written records.

The passage points to national restoration and future unity under the Messiah, the "one shepherd" who leads God's people in peace (Ezekiel 37:24–25, NLT). Scripture gives no indication that the sticks represent books or scrolls. Instead, the meaning is explicit and historical, and believers are warned not to insert private interpretations into prophecy: "No prophecy…came from the prophet's own understanding" (2 Peter 1:20, NLT).

MORMONISM

Mormon LDS doctrine teaches that the "stick of Judah" is the Bible and the "stick of Joseph" is the Book of Mormon, joined together as two scriptural witnesses (*Doctrine and Covenants 27:5; Book of Mormon Introduction*). This interpretation is not found in Ezekiel's text. The prophet explains the sticks as the two nations of Israel, not future scripture. The context centers on restored unity under one king, fulfilled in Christ, not the creation of additional sacred writings.

By assigning the "stick of Joseph" to the Book of Mormon, LDS teaching departs from the clear biblical meaning, adding an interpretation foreign to the passage. Scripture stands complete in its description of God restoring His people through the Messiah.

BAPTISMS FOR THE DEAD

CHRISTIANITY

As followers of Jesus Christ, Christians believe that salvation is found in Christ alone, through faith in Him, not through any ritual performed for those who have already died. Scripture is clear that "it is appointed unto men once to die, but after this the judgment" (Hebrews 9:27). Our time to accept Christ is in this life, not after death.

There is one brief mention in the Bible of people being "baptized for the dead" (1 Corinthians 15:29), but this verse is a descriptive reference, not a prescriptive command. Paul was pointing out the inconsistency of a practice that some in Corinth were doing, not endorsing it as a teaching of Jesus or the apostles. The rest of Scripture confirms that baptism is a personal act of obedience for the living believer, symbolizing their identification with Christ's death and resurrection (Romans 6:3–4).

MORMONISM

In contrast, *Mormonism* has built an entire temple system around performing baptisms and other ceremonies for the dead. Inside Mormon temples, members spend many hours researching the names of deceased people, often ancestors, and writing those names on small slips of paper. These names are then handed to someone who will act as a proxy, being immersed in water on behalf of each person.

It's common for one participant to be baptized for ten to fourteen deceased individuals in one session, or even many more if they personally found those names through genealogical work.

But that's not the only proxy work performed. Mormon temple rituals also include "marriages for the dead" and "sealings" that connect families eternally, concepts foreign to the teachings of Jesus and the apostles. Scripture warns us that "a great gulf is fixed" between the living and the dead, and "those who would pass from here to you cannot, nor can those from there pass to us" (Luke 16:26).

Doing religious work for the dead cannot change anyone's eternal destiny. Only faith in the living Christ saves. Anything that suggests otherwise distracts from the finished work of Jesus on the cross, who declared, "It is finished" (John 19:30).

GOD'S LOVE

CHRISTIANITY

As followers of Christ, we know that God's love is different from ours. His love is holy, pure, and unchanging. Our love, though sincere at times, is limited, conditional, and easily swayed by emotion or circumstance.

Scripture reminds us, "For my thoughts are not your thoughts, neither are your ways my ways," declares the Lord. "As the heavens are higher than the earth, so are my ways higher than your ways and my thoughts than your thoughts" (Isaiah 55:8–9).

When Jesus said, John 13:34 "...Love one another as I have loved you...," He wasn't asking us to love with our own love. He was asking us to love with His. That means the love we show others is meant to come from Him, through us, not from our human effort or understanding.

The only way to love like God is to let His Spirit love through us. When we surrender to His will, He changes the way we see people. His Spirit stretches us beyond what's comfortable and transforms our definition of love.

MORMONISM

In *Mormonism*, love often appears through service, family loyalty, or cheerful community life. But at its core, it is built on performance, not grace. Mormon doctrine teaches that worthiness and exaltation are achieved through works, obedience, and temple ordinances.

Without the indwelling of the Holy Spirit, the very presence of God's love within the heart, love becomes conditional. You may encounter outward kindness, but it's often shadowed by obligation, pressure, or confusion. Their teachings can contradict, and compassion is often limited by rules rather than released by grace.

When love is disconnected from truth, it becomes distorted. It can look sincere, but it lacks power. It may comfort the flesh but cannot heal the soul.

But God's love is altogether different. It is not earned—it is received. His love never manipulates, never demands, and never contradicts itself. It corrects with truth, comforts with mercy, and brings freedom wherever it flows.

Romans 5:5 declares, "God's love has been poured out into our hearts through the Holy Spirit, who has been given to us."

Those who do not know the true Jesus cannot love with His love. Release and forgive your Mormon friends.

SIN

CHRISTIANITY

In Christianity, sin is not merely the bad things we do, it is the condition of our hearts apart from God. It is our fallen nature, inherited through Adam, that separates us from the holiness of our Creator. Scripture teaches, "Surely I was sinful at birth, sinful from the time my mother conceived me" (Psalm 51:5).

Sin is the great divider. It is what makes us undeserving of God's presence. It doesn't just make us imperfect, it makes us spiritually dead. "For the wages of sin is death, but the gift of God is eternal life in Christ Jesus our Lord" (Romans 6:23).

The Bible doesn't say the "big" sins only, like murder or theft, lead to death. It says all sin does. Every lie, every prideful thought, every selfish motive, these reveal the corruption of the human heart. Without Jesus, every person stands guilty before a holy God.

But here's the good news: the Gospel isn't about what we do to overcome sin, it's about what Christ already did. Through His sacrifice on the cross, Jesus became the payment for our sin, once and for all.

He bridged the gulf that no amount of human effort could ever close.

True Christians understand that apart from Jesus, they deserve judgment. They know they cannot earn God's approval or "make up" for their wrongs through obedience or good works. Their confidence rests entirely on the finished work of Christ. That's why we rejoice in grace, it's the only reason we are saved at all.

Many Christians are surprised when they speak to Mormons and hear them agree with so much of what they say. Mormons will often affirm that Jesus is the Son of God, that He died for sin, that He rose again, and that grace is necessary for salvation. They even carry the Bible as part of their "quad"—a four-book set that includes the Book of Mormon, Doctrine and Covenants, and Pearl of Great Price.

So what's the difference?

The difference lies in definitions, a language barrier that hides an entirely different gospel.

My ex-Mormon Christian friend, Michael Flournoy, said it well:

> "Here is the question you must ask Latter-Day Saints: 'Are your current sins vile enough to justify God sending you to hell for eternity, despite whatever changes you've made in your life?'
> If the answer is no, then they are not Christian, because all true Christians know that their sins create an impossible gulf between them and God. They know that their hearts often desire that which is contrary to God's righteousness and that they deserve wrath. A true Christian rejoices in the gift of grace because they know the depth of the wound it covers."

MORMONISM

In *Mormonism*, sin is often viewed as mistakes to overcome or weaknesses to improve upon. Mormons believe that repentance, obedience, and temple ordinances help erase those sins over time. Grace, to them, is not a free and complete pardon, it's divine "help" given <u>after</u> they have done <u>all they can do</u>.

The Book of Mormon teaches, *"It is by grace that we are saved, <u>after</u> all we can do" (2 Nephi 25:23)*.

That single phrase changes everything. It takes grace, which Scripture declares to be a gift (Ephesians 2:8–9), and turns it into a reward for human effort. It replaces Christ's finished work with personal achievement.

In essence, Mormonism teaches that sin is not total depravity but temporary imperfection, something that can be corrected through obedience, endurance, and covenant faithfulness. But this denies the full power of the cross.

The Bible says, "If righteousness could be gained through the law, Christ died for nothing!" (Galatians 2:21).

PRAYER

CHRISTIANITY

In biblical Christianity, prayer is deeply personal, an open conversation between the believer and God the Father through Jesus Christ, empowered by the Holy Spirit. Jesus Himself taught us how to pray in Luke 11:2–4, saying:

> "Father, hallowed be Your name. Your kingdom come. Give us each day our daily bread. Forgive us our sins, for we also forgive everyone who sins against us. And lead us not into temptation."

This prayer reflects our direct access to God. We approach Him as children to a loving Father, honestly, humbly, and without ritual barriers. Prayer is not a performance or ceremony but a relationship. Philippians 4:6 reminds us:

> "Don't worry about anything; instead, pray about everything. Tell God what you need, and thank Him for all He has done."

God invites us to come as we are, whether broken, crying, or confused, and to speak to Him personally. He listens, comforts, and gives peace that surpasses understanding (Philippians 4:7).

MORMONISM

In *Mormon* temple ceremonies, however, prayer is not approached as a personal conversation with God but as a structured group ritual tied to worthiness and temple ordinances. During the temple "True Order of Prayer," women are required to veil their faces while men lead the prayer. Participants repeat the words of the man praying as names from a bag are mentioned before God.

This ritualistic prayer stands in contrast to the biblical invitation to pray directly to God, freely and personally. Jesus never instructed women to veil themselves in prayer or for believers to repeat after a man.

2 Corinthians 3:13-16 NLT, "We are not like Moses, who put a veil over his face so the people of Israel would not see the glory, even though it was destined to fade away. But the people's minds were hardened, and to this day whenever the old covenant is being read, the same veil covers their minds so they cannot understand the truth. And this veil can be removed only by believing in Christ. Yes, even today when they read Moses' writings, their hearts are covered with that veil, and they do not understand. But whenever someone turns to the Lord, the veil is taken away.

Jesus taught that all who believe in Him have equal access to the Father, as children of God, not as participants in a secret ceremony.

THE SABBATH DAY, HOLY SET APART

CHRISTIANITY

In biblical Christianity, the Sabbath points to rest in Christ, not merely rest from work. Under the Old Covenant, the Sabbath was the seventh day of the week, a day of physical rest commanded by God after His six days of creation (Exodus 20:8–11). But in the New Covenant, Jesus fulfills the Sabbath law. He declares Himself to be "Lord of the Sabbath" (Matthew 12:8), meaning that true rest is now found in Him, not in a single day of ritual observance.

Christians gather on Sunday, the Lord's Day, not as a strict replacement of the Jewish Sabbath, but in celebration of Jesus' resurrection. Early believers met on this day to break bread, pray, and hear the apostles' teaching (Acts 20:7; 1 Corinthians 16:2).

The heart of the Christian Sabbath is not about rules or restrictions, but relationship and renewal, a time to worship, rest, and enjoy fellowship with God and His people. Hebrews 4:9–10 reminds us,

"There remains, then, a Sabbath rest for the people of God; for anyone who enters God's rest also rests from their works, just as God did from His."

This means we no longer strive to earn righteousness by outward observance. Our rest is spiritual, trusting in the finished work of Christ rather than our own efforts.

MORMONISM

In *Mormonism*, Sunday observance holds a far more ritualistic and behavioral significance. The Sabbath is not simply a day of worship but a day of proving worthiness through obedience. Attendance at Sunday meetings is viewed as essential to remaining "unspotted from the world," as stated in their scripture *Doctrine and Covenants 59:9:*

"And that thou mayest more fully keep thyself unspotted from the world, thou shalt go to the house of prayer and offer up thy sacraments upon my holy day."

The Mormon Sabbath revolves around the weekly sacrament, which is believed to wash away sins committed during the week. While missing a weekday youth activity might not be a big deal, missing Sunday services is serious. It is seen as a spiritual failure or sign of disobedience.

HOME CHURCH

CHRISTIANITY

In biblical Christianity, belonging to a church is not about being assigned by location or tracked through membership numbers, it's about being led by the Holy Spirit into a community of believers where you can grow, serve, and worship together.

Scripture teaches that the Church is the body of Christ (1 Corinthians 12:12–27), and every believer is a member of that body through faith in Jesus, not through administrative assignment. Christians prayerfully seek a local congregation where they can fellowship, receive teaching, and participate in ministry. This process is guided by God, not by man-made boundaries or record systems.

Hebrews 10:25 NLT, "Let us not neglect our meeting together, as some people do, but encourage one another–especially now that the day of his return is drawing near."

While local churches may have processes for joining or serving, there is no centralized record keeping or numerical tracking of members' tithing or attendance. Giving is an act of personal worship, done freely and cheerfully as 2 Corinthians 9:7 says:

"Each one must give as he has decided in his heart, not reluctantly or under compulsion, for God loves a cheerful giver."

Leadership within the church also follows biblical principles of calling, training, and discernment. Paul warns Timothy in 1 Timothy 5:22:

"Never be in a hurry about appointing a church leader. Do not share in the sins of others. Keep yourself pure."

This means pastors, elders, and teachers must be tested, trained, and proven faithful, grounded deeply in Scripture and mature in faith. They are to lead by example, not by authority or control.

In many Christian churches, leaders intentionally raise up future shepherds and disciplers, fulfilling the Great Commission (Matthew 28:19–20). Healthy churches equip believers to lead others to Christ and make disciples who will one day lead too. Leadership is seen as servanthood, not status.

MORMONISM

In the *Mormon* church, membership is highly structured and administrative. Every member is assigned to a specific ward (local congregation) based strictly on geographical boundaries. These ward lines are determined by the church organization, not personal choice.

When Mormons move to a new location, they look up their new ward using the church's online boundary map to find the correct meetinghouse and service times. If they attend a ward outside their assigned area, they typically need special permission from their local stake president, and their membership records must be officially transferred to the new ward.

Each individual is given a membership ID number, usually assigned at baptism, which is used to track their church records, participation, tithing, and callings. Much like a customer membership number, this system helps church authorities manage data and ensure compliance with expected duties. Bishops and stake leaders review tithing during annual interviews, where members declare whether they are full or partial tithe payers, a factor that can determine their worthiness to enter LDS temples.

This administrative approach contrasts sharply with the freedom of the believer in Christ found in biblical Christianity. Rather than following the Spirit's personal leading to find a church home, Mormons are expected to stay within their assigned boundaries, attend their designated ward, and submit to the hierarchical structure of leadership that begins with bishops and extends up to the president and apostles in Salt Lake City.

LEADERSHIP

Biblical Christianity presents leadership as a calling shaped by the Holy Spirit rather than a ladder of advancement. The New Testament offers a simple structure rooted in shepherding and service. Pastors guide the flock through teaching and spiritual care (Ephesians 4:11, NLT). Teachers explain Scripture with clarity and faithfulness, recognizing that those who instruct are judged more strictly (James 3:1, NLT). Elders, also called overseers, are mature believers who guard doctrine and model humility for the church (1 Peter 5:1–3, NLT). Deacons support the ministry through faithful service to practical needs (1 Timothy 3:8–13, NLT). Evangelists proclaim the gospel wherever God sends them, helping the church grow in discernment and faith (Ephesians 4:11, NLT).

Biblical leadership is never presented as a series of levels or ranks. Instead, it is a spiritual stewardship grounded in character, maturity, and calling. Jesus warned His disciples against pursuing status or hierarchy, saying, "The greatest among you must be a servant" (Matthew 23:11, NLT). Authority comes from Scripture and the Spirit, not from ascending through offices or achieving worthiness. Every believer is called to test teaching by the Word of God, for true leadership always points away from self and toward Christ. As Paul writes, "Test everything that is said. Hold on to what is good" (1 Thessalonians 5:21, NLT).

Within this biblical framework, the church functions as a body, not a bureaucracy. Pastors, teachers, elders, deacons, and evangelists work together to build up the people of God, each role serving the others. Leadership is defined by humility and sacrifice, not position or progression, and it stands in contrast to systems that create spiritual hierarchy or divide believers into levels of authority.

MORMONISM

Mormonism approaches leadership through a structured hierarchy built on priesthood authority, age-based advancement, and graded offices. From childhood through adulthood, every member moves through an organized system of titles and responsibilities viewed as steps toward spiritual progression.

In the LDS Young Women's program, girls advance through a sequence of age-assigned identities: Beehive at twelve, Mia Maid at fourteen, and Laurel at sixteen. Each group forms its own presidency, a president with counselors and a secretary, creating leadership positions not rooted in spiritual calling but in organizational structure. These roles, while meaningful within LDS culture, reflect a system of progression rather than the biblical pattern of Spirit-given gifts.

The Young Men's program introduces boys to the Aaronic Priesthood through a series of offices given at preset ages. A twelve-year-old becomes a Deacon, a fourteen-year-old becomes a Teacher, and a sixteen-year-old becomes a Priest (*Gospel Principles*). In LDS belief, these are not symbolic roles but actual priesthood authority that allows young teenagers to perform ordinances such as preparing or passing the sacrament and even baptizing. This mirrors no biblical pattern, for Scripture never assigns priestly authority to youth, and the biblical office of deacon bears no resemblance to an age-based appointment.

Adulthood brings further division within the LDS priesthood system. Men enter the Melchizedek Priesthood, where they become Elders, and later High Priests, depending on calling and worthiness. Leadership expands into bishoprics composed of a bishop and his counselors, while higher positions include Seventies, Apostles, and the First Presidency. In LDS theology, these leaders hold priesthood keys that regulate ordinances believed necessary for spiritual advancement and covenant progression. The prophet is considered God's mouthpiece on earth, whose declarations carry binding authority.

This system stands in clear contrast to the biblical model. In Christianity, an elder and a pastor share the same role, and no higher priesthood exists beyond the finished work of Christ. Leadership is not tied to salvation or the administration of essential ordinances. No believer holds exclusive keys to mediate divine favor, for Scripture teaches that every Christian has direct access to God through Jesus.

Where the Bible centers leadership on calling, character, and spiritual gifting, Mormonism centers leadership on age, rank, and priesthood hierarchy. Where Christianity emphasizes discernment and submission to Scripture, Mormonism emphasizes obedience to leaders who claim continuing revelation. The difference is not merely organizational but theological, shaping how authority is understood and how spiritual life is pursued.

EVANGELISTS AND MISSIONARIES

CHRISTIANITY

In Christianity, believers are called by God and given divine purpose: to prophesy, evangelize, and share the good news of salvation through Jesus Christ. This is known as the Great Commission:

Matthew 28:19–20 (ESV)
"Go therefore and make disciples of all nations, baptizing them in the name of the Father and of the Son and of the Holy Spirit, teaching them to observe all that I have commanded you."

The Holy Spirit empowers the Christian mission:

Acts 1:8 (ESV)
"But you will receive power when the Holy Spirit has come upon you, and you will be my witnesses in Jerusalem and in all Judea and Samaria, and to the end of the earth."

God continues to call and send His people today:

Acts 13:2–3 (ESV)
"Set apart for me Barnabas and Saul for the work to which I have called them."

And He gives spiritual gifts and callings to equip His Church:

Ephesians 4:11–12 (ESV)

"And He gave the apostles, the prophets, the evangelists, the shepherds and teachers, to equip the saints for the work of ministry, for building up the body of Christ."

The calling of the evangelist continues today, proclaiming the gospel (In the Greek, the word Gospel is "euangelion", meaning "good news" or "to announce glad tidings").

The Good News is that Jesus Christ died for our sins, was buried, and rose again, offering eternal life by grace through faith to all who believe (1 Corinthians 15:3–4; Ephesians 2:8–9).

Romans 10:15 (ESV)
"How beautiful are the feet of those who bring good news!"

MORMONISM

In *Mormonism*, missionary work operates very differently from biblical evangelism.

Young men, at age 18, are expected to serve a two-year mission wherever they are assigned by church leadership, through a letter from the LDS Prophet. Young women may serve 18-month missions starting at age 19, a shorter period due to the church's <u>emphasis</u> on early marriage and <u>childbearing</u> as their <u>primary calling</u> (used to be age 21, and there is talk of lowering the age to 18).

Missionaries are trained using a manual titled "Preach My Gospel." Their purpose is to convert others to Mormonism, teaching that salvation comes through obedience to LDS commandments, temple rituals, and works, not by grace alone through faith in Christ.

These teachings include ideas such as eternal marriage, "forever families," and performing baptisms and marriages for the dead so that deceased ancestors can "accept the gospel" in the afterlife, doctrines not found in the Bible:

"Give priority to Book of Mormon passages when you teach…. The Bible and Book of Mormon complement and enrich each other" (Preach My Gospel, What Is the Role of the Book of Mormon, 2018, cht. 5).

Mormon Missionaries begin teaching investigators the Book of Mormon as their hook, and later introduce the other books they believe in:

Mormon Scripture: Doctrine and Covenants 132:19–20

"If a man marry a wife by my word… and it is sealed unto them by the Holy Spirit of promise… then shall they be gods, because they have no end; therefore shall they be from everlasting to everlasting."

Doctrine and Covenants 128:17–18

"The salvation of the dead is necessary and essential… for their deliverance, that they may be judged according to men in the flesh, but live according to God in the spirit… For we without them cannot be made perfect; neither can they without us be made perfect."

However, we know the Bible warns that any message that adds to or changes the gospel of Jesus Christ (Grace) is not from God:

Galatians 1:6–8 (ESV)
"I am astonished that you are so quickly deserting him who called you in the grace of Christ and are turning to a different gospel, not that there is another one, but there are some who trouble you and want to distort the gospel of Christ.

But even if we or an angel from heaven should preach to you a gospel contrary to the one we preached to you, let him be accursed."

SUPERNATURAL GOD

In biblical Christianity, God is not a being confined by time, space, or matter. He is eternal Spirit, all-powerful, all-knowing, and sovereign over the very laws He created. The God of Scripture does not merely work within the natural world; He transcends it. Every miracle throughout the Bible reveals His divine authority over creation itself. God is Spirit, Not Flesh.

Jesus declared, "God is Spirit, and those who worship Him must worship in spirit and truth" (John 4:24). When the risen Christ appeared to His disciples, He said, "A spirit does not have flesh and bones as you see that I have" (Luke 24:39). (This verse is about Jesus' resurrected body, not about the eternal nature of God the Father.)

These verses reveal that God is supernatural by His very nature, not bound by the physical realm or limited to a body of flesh and bone. He is the Creator, existing outside and above the created order.

The miracles of Scripture are not natural occurrences that can be explained away. They are divine interruptions of the ordinary, meant to reveal the extraordinary power of the living God. In Mark 3:5, Jesus instantly healed a man's withered hand. In John 11:43, He raised Lazarus from the dead. In Mark 6:49, He walked on water, defying gravity itself. In John 20:19, He appeared through locked doors to comfort His disciples. And in 2

Kings 13:21, even Elisha's bones brought a man back to life when they touched his body.

Each of these events points to a God who commands creation, not one who operates within its limits. He is Lord over all, not subject to the laws of physics or nature.

God Dwells in His People, not in temples.

The Bible is equally clear that God no longer dwells in manmade structures. "The Most High does not dwell in houses made by hands," says Acts 7:48–49. "Heaven is My throne, and the earth is My footstool." Instead, under the New Covenant, His Spirit resides within His people. Paul wrote, "Your body is a temple of the Holy Spirit who is in you" (1 Corinthians 6:19).

This truth changes everything. God is not limited to a building, an ordinance, or a ceremony. His presence fills His church, the living, breathing body of believers redeemed by the blood of Christ. The God of the Bible is wholly supernatural, beyond all human limitation, yet personally present within every heart that calls Him Lord.

MORMONISM

In contrast, the *Mormons* describe a very different kind of deity. Mormon theology presents God not as an eternal, supernatural Spirit, but as an exalted man, a being who lives within the boundaries of time and space. While Mormons acknowledge miracles and divine acts, their concept of God and heaven is naturalized and human-centered, not transcendent as revealed in Scripture. They believe God has a body of flesh and bone.

From Mormon scripture *D&C 130:22, "The Father has a body of flesh and bones as tangible as man's; the Son also; but the Holy Ghost has not a body of flesh and bones, but is a personage of Spirit."*

This statement directly opposes the words of Jesus in John 4:24, that God is Spirit. In LDS belief, God exists within the created order, bound by physical form. Rather than being the infinite Creator beyond matter and time, He is portrayed as part of it.

Joseph Smith taught, *"God himself was once as we are now, and is an exalted man, and sits enthroned in yonder heavens" (Teachings of the Prophet Joseph Smith, p. 345).* This concept, that God was once a mortal who became divine, stands in sharp contrast to Scripture, which teaches that God has always been God. "From everlasting to everlasting, You are God" (Psalm 90:2), and "I the Lord do not change" (Malachi 3:6).

The God of the Bible did not evolve, progress, or ascend. He simply is the eternal "I AM" (Exodus 3:14).

In LDS scripture, this belief extends to humanity itself: *"Then shall they be gods, because they have no end; therefore shall they be from everlasting to everlasting" (Doctrine and Covenants 132:20).*

But the Bible never teaches that humans can become divine. Scripture reveals that believers are adopted into God's family as His children (Romans 8:14–17). Through Christ, we are made partakers of His divine nature (2 Peter 1:4), but we do not share His divine essence. We are redeemed, not deified. We are made new creations, not new gods.

Mormon scripture commands, *"Organize yourselves; prepare every needful thing; and establish a house, even a house of prayer, a house of fasting, a house of faith"* (Doctrine and Covenants 88:119). While this emphasizes spiritual devotion, it also reflects a continued dependence on physical temples for communion with God.

In contrast, the New Testament teaches that God no longer resides in temples made by men (Acts 7:48). His presence now indwells His people through the Holy Spirit (1 Corinthians 6:19). No longer must humanity build physical structures to meet Him. The true temple of God is within the believer.

Although Mormonism acknowledges miracles and divine manifestations, these are often presented as extensions of human authority, performed through priesthood power or keys, rather than as demonstrations of a God who exists above nature itself. The focus shifts from "God alone can" to "we can, through eternal progression."

In this way, the supernatural power of God is subtly replaced by the natural potential of man. The LDS path to divinity becomes a human-centered journey upward, rather than a divine act of grace reaching downward.

PREEXISTENCE MORMON FALSE TEACHING

CHRISTIANITY

Biblical Christianity teaches that human beings did not exist before birth. Life begins when God creates each person in the womb. Psalm 139:13–16 says God knits us together before birth, and Zechariah 12:1 declares that the Lord "forms the human spirit within a person." Scripture is clear about the order of creation: "It is sown a natural body, it is raised a spiritual body… The spiritual did not come first, but the natural, and after that the spiritual" (1 Corinthians 15:44–47). Humanity is first physical, then spiritual through new birth in Christ (John 3:3–7).

The Bible also reveals that Jesus is eternal God, not a created being. "In the beginning was the Word, and the Word was with God, and the Word was God" (John 1:1). He is the Creator of all things, including angels (Colossians 1:16), and is not equal to them. Satan, by contrast, is a fallen angel who rebelled against God (Isaiah 14:12–15; Luke 10:18). The Bible contains no record of Jesus and Satan being "spirit brothers", or of a heavenly council, spirit siblings, or competing salvation plans.

MORMONISM

In contrast, *Mormonism* teaches that all people existed as spirit children of Heavenly Father and Heavenly Mother before being born on earth. Mormons often cite "I knew you before you were in your mother's womb" (Jer.

1:5), but in relation to pre-mortal life, instead of God's foreknowledge. In *LDS* belief, this pre-mortal life was a time when each spirit waited for the chance to receive a physical body and prove worthy of exaltation. Their teachings come from extra-biblical writings such as the Book of Abraham (*Abraham 3:22-23*), Book of Moses (Moses 3-4), and Doctrine and Covenants (*D&C 93:29; 138:55-56*), not from the Holy Bible.

Mormonism also teaches that Jesus and Lucifer were spirit brothers who both presented plans of salvation to God the Father (*Moses 4:1-4; Abraham 3:27-28*). Jesus' plan supposedly upheld free will, while Lucifer's plan forced obedience. It is taught when the Father chose Jesus' plan, Lucifer rebelled and became Satan. This idea has no biblical foundation and directly contradicts Scripture, which identifies Satan as a created being, not divine. In Mormon theology, God Himself was once a man who progressed to godhood, and faithful Mormons may likewise become gods over their own worlds. This belief opposes Isaiah 43:10, where God declares, "Before me no god was formed, nor will there be one after me."

PRIESTHOOD

CHRISTIANITY

Hebrews 7:11–12 teaches that perfection could never come through the Levitical priesthood; therefore, a new priest arose, **Jesus Christ**, after the order of Melchizedek. In biblical Christianity, the priesthood was fulfilled and finished in Christ, our eternal High Priest. This priesthood is <u>unchangeable</u> and non-transferrable (Hebrews 7:24). The Greek word used here is "aparabatos", meaning "untransferable, permanent, not liable to pass to a successor." This word is significant because it is a hapax legomenon, a term used only once in all of scripture.

The Old Testament priests offered sacrifices for sin, but Jesus became both the final Priest and the perfect Sacrifice (1 Timothy 2:5; Hebrews 10:10–14). Through Him, every believer is now part of a royal priesthood (1 Peter 2:9), able to approach God directly without human mediators. When he died, the veil was torn.

MORMONISM

In *Mormonism*, the priesthood is viewed as the literal authority and power of God, granted to worthy male members of the Church to act in His name. Latter-day Saints teach that all ordinances necessary for salvation, such as baptism, confirmation, temple marriage, and blessing the sacrament, must be performed by someone who holds this priesthood authority. Without it, they believe no act of worship or covenant is valid before God.

Mormon doctrine divides this authority into two priesthoods:

1. The Aaronic Priesthood – Called the lesser priesthood, it is said to hold *"the keys of the ministering of angels"* and the preparatory gospel *(Doctrine and Covenants 84:26)*. It is conferred/transferred onto worthy boys, usually beginning at age 12, to prepare them for higher authority.
2. The Melchizedek Priesthood – Considered the higher priesthood, is believed to hold *"the keys of all the spiritual blessings of the Church"* *(Doctrine and Covenants 107:18)*. This authority includes performing confirmations, ordaining others, giving blessings, leading congregations, and performing temple ordinances. Adult men deemed "worthy" are ordained to this priesthood.

Mormonism teaches that these priesthoods were lost after the deaths of Christ's apostles and later restored to Joseph Smith by heavenly beings. According to LDS scripture, John the Baptist appeared to Smith and Oliver Cowdery in 1829 and restored the Aaronic Priesthood (Doctrine and Covenants 13). Shortly after, Peter, James, and John allegedly appeared and bestowed upon them the Melchizedek Priesthood.

This belief in a restored priesthood is central to the LDS faith. It undergirds their claim that the Church of Jesus Christ of Latter-day Saints is the only true church on earth, because, in their view, it alone possesses the authority to act in God's name. All other churches are seen as lacking divine authority.

Mormonism strives to replace grace with effort, truth with secrecy, and the eternal priesthood of Christ with a man-made system. Christianity rests in the finished work of Jesus, the only High Priest who saves completely. There is no restoration needed, no secret knowledge required. His gospel is full, final, and forever.

WOMEN

CHRISTIANITY

In biblical Christianity, a woman's value and calling come directly from God, not from her husband, church leadership, or religious performance.

The woman described in Proverbs 31 is strong, wise, and industrious. She is: A merchant who trades and conducts business, a provider who invests in land and plants vineyards, a caregiver whose lamp does not go out at night because she works diligently for her household, a woman of strength, clothed in dignity, who laughs without fear of the future.

Christian theology teaches that the same Holy Spirit lives in both men and women. Women have authority in Christ to pray for the sick (James 5:14–16). They are free to prophesy, teach, and serve as the Spirit leads (Acts 2:17–18, Galatians 3:28). They are partners in grace, not subordinates in worth (1 Peter 3:7).

The Christian woman's purpose is to love God first, and through that love, serve her family and community with strength, compassion, and wisdom. She is not limited to the home, she is empowered by God to live out her calling wherever He leads.

MORMONISM

In contrast, *Mormonism* teaches women to aim high in choosing a husband who meets specific church qualifications. From a young age, LDS girls are influenced that their eternal progression depends on marrying a worthy priesthood holder (*Doctrines of the Gospel, i.e. D&C 132:7, 15-18)*), a man who: Has served a full two-year mission, obeys all church standards and temple requirements, holds priesthood authority and can "lead" his family spiritually.

Women are told that only through such a husband can they enter the Mormon temple and reach the highest level of heaven (the Celestial Kingdom).

The LDS Relief Society, founded by Emma Smith under Joseph Smith's direction in 1842, was created to "relieve" men of temporal burdens so they could focus on their priesthood duties. In the Nauvoo Relief Society minutes, Joseph Smith is recorded as saying the purpose of the society was to "assist; by correcting the morals and strengthening the virtues of the female community, and save the Elders the trouble of rebuking; that they may give their time to other duties…" (The Church of Jesus Christ of Latter-day Saints, n.d.-a).

It grew rather quickly and now stands as one of the largest women's groups in the world with 7 million members in over 188 countries and territories. In practice, this reinforced the idea that men are the spiritual leaders who hear from God, while women fend for themselves and support the men in their (much more important) duties.

Women in the LDS faith are: Encouraged to pursue education, yet expected to stay home as full-time nurturers, not permitted to anoint the sick with oil or exercise priesthood authority, taught from infancy that their primary role is to nurture children and support their husband's priesthood service. While they are often dedicated mothers and capable leaders, their spiritual authority is limited to what their husbands or male leaders delegate to them.

FASTING & OFFERING

CHRISTIANITY

Fasting and offering are both acts of worship, but in Scripture they serve different spiritual purposes. Fasting is a time of humbling ourselves before God, denying the flesh to seek spiritual breakthrough and dependence on Him. Jesus taught that some spiritual victories require both prayer and fasting:

> "Jesus replied, 'This kind can be cast out only by prayer and fasting'" (Mark 9:29, NLT). Through fasting, believers grow in spiritual authority, clarity, and self-discipline, learning to hear God's voice above the noise of the flesh. Offerings, however, are an act of sacrifice and generosity, giving back to God from what He has already given.
> "You must each decide in your heart how much to give. And don't give reluctantly or in response to pressure. 'For God loves a person who gives cheerfully'" (2 Corinthians 9:7, NLT). Offerings are not commanded as a duty tied to fasting, but as freewill gifts motivated by love and gratitude. The Bible teaches that giving should never be coerced, but guided by the Holy Spirit.

MORMONISM

In *Mormonism*, Fast Sunday occurs on the first Sunday of each month. Members are instructed to abstain from two meals and donate the money saved to the church as a fast offering. Young men, often holding the Aaronic

Priesthood, collect these donations door-to-door that same day. While this practice appears charitable, it combines two separate biblical acts, fasting and offering, into one institutional ritual. The Church of Jesus Christ of Latter-day Saints (LDS) General Handbook states:

> "Members are encouraged to fast for two consecutive meals, and to give at least the value of the meals not eaten as a fast offering to help those in need" (General Handbook, 34.1.3).

This blurs the distinction between fasting as private devotion and offering as voluntary giving, making the act more structured than Spirit-led. True biblical fasting is a private matter between the believer and God (Matthew 6:16–18, NLT), not a ritual linked to financial giving or overseen by human authority.

THE CREATION

CHRISTIANITY

The Bible begins with a clear declaration:

> "In the beginning God created the heavens and the earth. The earth was formless and empty, and darkness covered the deep waters. And the Spirit of God was hovering over the surface of the waters. Then God said, 'Let there be light,' and there was light" (Genesis 1:1–3, NLT).

The Hebrew word for create, 'bara' (בָּרָא, H1254), means "to bring into existence from nothing." The word for formless, 'tohu' (תֹּהוּ, H8414), means "emptiness" or "wasteland." This shows that God did not shape pre-existing matter but spoke creation into being ex nihilo, "out of nothing" (Psalm 33:6; Romans 4:17).

All things were created by Him and for Him:

> "For through him God created everything in the heavenly realms and on earth. He made the things we can see and the things we can't see… Everything was created through him and for him" (Colossians 1:16, NLT).

The Bible presents God as the sole Creator, not an organizer of chaotic material. His Word alone holds creative power.

Sin entered the world through Adam's disobedience, not through a "noble" act of enlightenment.

> "When Adam sinned, sin entered the world. Adam's sin brought death, so death spread to everyone" (Romans 5:12, NLT).

This event separated humanity from God, but redemption came through Christ:

> "Just as everyone dies because we all belong to Adam, everyone who belongs to Christ will be given new life" (1 Corinthians 15:22, NLT).

In Greek, create (κτίζω, ktizō) means "to found, to establish, to make." God is both the origin and sustainer of creation, Theos Pantokratōr, "God Almighty."

Christian theology affirms: God created out of nothing (ex nihilo), Adam's sin brought death, not enlightenment, Jesus Christ, the "last Adam" (1 Corinthians 15:45), brought life and restoration, and God reveals truth freely to those who seek Him through the Holy Spirit (1 Corinthians 2:10, NLT).

MORMONISM

In *Mormonism*, the Creation Video shown in LDS temples portrays Adam and Eve as noble figures who had to partake of the forbidden fruit to bring about human knowledge and godhood. This aligns with the LDS doctrine that humanity can "progress to become gods."

The Book of Moses 5:11 (Pearl of Great Price) states:

> *"And Eve, his wife, heard all these things and was glad, saying: Were it not for our transgression we never*

should have had seed, and never should have known good and evil."

The Second Article of Faith reads:

"We believe that men will be punished for their own sins, and not for Adam's transgression."

This teaching denies original sin and redefines the Fall as a necessary step toward exaltation.

Furthermore, LDS doctrine teaches that God "organized" the world from pre-existing matter:

"The earth was not created from nothing; rather, it was organized from existing matter" (Doctrine and Covenants 93:29–33).

The word organize in the LDS text implies rearrangement, not divine creation. This conflicts directly with the biblical term bara' (create), which means to bring forth what did not exist.

The LDS Church also teaches that Michael became Adam, who helped form the earth before becoming human (Temple Endowment Narrative). This contradicts Scripture, which identifies God alone as Creator (Isaiah 45:18).

By teaching that humans can eventually become gods, Mormonism exalts creation over the Creator, a concept the Bible condemns (Romans 1:25).

THE LAW

The Law was never meant to save us, it was meant to expose our need for salvation. Scripture says, "For no one can ever be made right with God by doing what the law commands. The law simply shows us how sinful we are" (Romans 3:20, NLT).

The commandments reveal our inability to reach perfection on our own. They humble the self-righteous heart that says, "I can do this! I can please the Father!" Until we realize that the Law was designed to break us, not to shame us, but to bring us to Jesus, we remain bound by striving.

God's Word continues: "But now God has shown us a way to be made right with him without keeping the requirements of the law… We are made right with God by placing our faith in Jesus Christ" (Romans 3:21–22, NLT). The phrase "a way" does not refer to a human plan or a set of steps—it refers to a Person. Jesus said, "I am the way, the truth, and the life" (John 14:6, NLT).

Jesus did not come to abolish the Law but to fulfill it: "Don't misunderstand why I have come. I did not come to abolish the law of Moses or the writings of the prophets. No, I came to accomplish their purpose" (Matthew 5:17, NLT).

The Law exposes sin; Christ completes what we could not. Faith in Him brings righteousness now, not someday after perfection. Works then become the fruit of salvation, not the requirement for it. As James wrote, "Just as the body is dead without breath, so also faith is dead without good works" (James 2:26, NLT). The gospel is not about climbing higher, it's about surrendering to the One who already reached down.

MORMONISM

In *Mormonism*, the Law is not primarily a mirror to reveal sin but a ladder toward exaltation. The Church of Jesus Christ of Latter-day Saints teaches that additional scripture, The Book of Mormon, Doctrine and Covenants, and The Pearl of Great Price, completes what the Bible began. These writings present commandments, ordinances, and covenants as continuing steps toward becoming like God.

According to LDS belief, salvation includes faith in Jesus Christ but also obedience to commandments, baptism, temple ordinances, and lifelong covenant keeping. As *Doctrine and Covenants 76 and 2 Nephi 25:23* explain, grace operates *"after all we can do."* In this system, grace assists the obedient rather than saves the helpless.

While The Family: A Proclamation to the World emphasizes eternal marriage and family sealings as essential to God's plan, the Bible teaches that eternal life is found only in union with Christ, not through earthly ordinances.

The difference is simple yet eternal: the gospel says, "It is finished." Religion says, "Keep climbing."

CHANGE

CHRISTIANITY

Scripture reveals a God who does not change. "I am the Lord, and I do not change" (Malachi 3:6, NLT). His character, His purposes, and His nature remain constant. He is the one true God, not one among many, and certainly not a being who produces additional gods. "The Lord is God, and there is no other" (Deuteronomy 4:35, NLT).

God graciously calls His people His children: "But to all who believed him and accepted him, he gave the right to become children of God" (John 1:12, NLT). This adoption is a gift of grace, not the result of human progression into godhood. Scripture insists that God is utterly unlike man: "God is not a man, so he does not lie. He is not human, so he does not change his mind" (Numbers 23:19, NLT). Jesus Himself "did not trust them, because he knew human nature. No one needed to tell him what mankind is really like" (John 2:24–25, NLT).

The Fall revealed how deeply we need Him, not how close we are to becoming divine. Jesus declared, "Apart from me you can do nothing" (John 15:5, NLT). What is impossible for man is possible with God alone (Matthew 19:26). We fall short, we change, we contradict ourselves, but God remains steady, true, and eternally faithful. Only He is worthy of trust.

MORMONISM

Mormon Joseph Smith's accounts of his First Vision illustrate a pattern opposite of God's unchanging nature. According to the official LDS Church essay, his descriptions of the event shifted significantly over time. In 1832, Smith recorded seeing a single heavenly figure. In 1835, he described a "multitude of angels." By 1838, his narrative changed again, this time claiming he saw two divine beings, identified as the Father and the Son, one pointing to the other and saying, "This is my beloved Son. Hear Him." This version became the canonized account in *Pearl of Great Price (Joseph Smith History 1:17)*. These differences are documented directly in LDS sources.

The phrase "This is my beloved Son; hear him" does not originate with Joseph Smith's experience. It comes from Scripture, spoken by God the Father at the Mount of Transfiguration (Luke 9:35, KJV). The origin of the phrase is biblical, not Latter-day Saint. Feelings of reverence that arise when hearing those words belong rightly to God's revelation, not to Joseph Smith's retellings.

LDS doctrine also adapts across time, reflecting continual adjustment rather than the biblical picture of a fixed, eternal faith delivered once for all (Jude 1:3). Even garments, initially long, full-body underclothing, have been repeatedly redesigned to match social expectations. The missionary age requirements are also being adjusted, as are the rules of contact for the missionary. This pattern of doctrinal and practical alteration stands in sharp contrast to the God of Scripture, who does not change and whose Word remains forever.

THE PAST

The past is an amazing place to learn from, but a terrible place to live in. God calls His people to look ahead. "Remember ye not the former things, neither consider the things of old." (Isaiah 43:18 KJV), "For I am about to do something new. See, I have already begun! Do you not see it?" (Isaiah 43:19, NLT).

Through Christ, we receive new beginnings every day. Scripture declares, "So now there is no condemnation for those who belong to Christ Jesus" (Romans 8:1, NLT). "...his mercies begin afresh each morning." (Lamentations 3:23 NLT). The weight of past failure is lifted because Jesus fulfilled what the Law demanded. We are no longer bound by shame but renewed through grace.

When we set goals or start fresh seasons, it can feel like a surge of life, almost as if the victory has already been achieved. Spiritually, this mirrors God's promise: "You can pray for anything, and if you have faith, you will receive it" (Matthew 21:22, NLT). The hope we feel when we trust His Word is the Holy Spirit reminding us that God's promises are already secure in Christ.

Jesus, the perfect One, saved us completely. He not only forgives the past but re-creates us. "This means that anyone who belongs to Christ has become a new person. The old life is gone; a new life has begun!" (2 Corinthians 5:17, NLT).

For those leaving behind religious systems that once defined your faith, including temple covenants or legalistic frameworks, God offers rest. Your marriage, your family, and your future are not lost, they can now be grounded in truth. A Christ-centered marriage is no longer bound by ritual but strengthened by a threefold cord, husband, wife, and the Holy Spirit (Ecclesiastes 4:12, NLT).

The Bible teaches that God is faithful and trustworthy: "Trust in the Lord with all your heart; do not depend on your own understanding. Seek his will in all you do, and he will show you which path to take" (Proverbs 3:5-6, NLT). He is not a man that He should lie (Numbers 23:19, NLT). He provides for His children just as He cares for the sparrows (Matthew 6:26, NLT).

God's grace wipes away your past, it does not demand that you keep rewriting it. When you come to Christ, you are not working toward forgiveness; you are living from it. His mercy renews your future and replaces guilt with peace.

MORMONISM

In *Mormonism* theology, grace is often described as a helping power that comes only *"after all we can do" (2 Nephi 25:23, Book of Mormon)*. This framework leads to continual striving, an endless cycle of repentance and recommitment where sin feels never fully removed. Forgiveness is viewed as conditional upon personal effort and worthiness, rather than a finished gift of Christ.

Mormon culture also places heavy emphasis on genealogy and ancestral connection. While remembering family is honorable, the constant focus on past generations and temple ordinances can anchor believers to what was, rather than freeing them for what God is doing now. By contrast, THE BIBLE calls us to "forget the past and look forward to what lies ahead" (Philippians 3:13, NLT).

Ultimately, Mormonism teaches progression toward perfection through personal obedience, whereas the Bible teaches salvation by grace through faith alone (Ephesians 2:8-9, NLT). The gospel frees believers from striving; it replaces endless self-cleansing with Christ's once-for-all redemption.

PROPHETIC WORDS VS PATRIARCHAL BLESSINGS

CHRISTIANITY

In Scripture, God speaks to His people through His Word and, at times, through prophetic encouragement that aligns with Scripture. The New Testament shows believers receiving Spirit-led guidance that strengthens their faith, always pointing back to Christ and never replacing the authority of Scripture. Paul writes, "And I am certain that God, who began the good work within you, will continue his work until it is finally finished on the day when Christ Jesus returns" (Phil 1:6, NLT). The Christian life is not shaped by a single predetermined roadmap but by the ongoing work of Christ, unfolding through daily obedience as God leads.

Prophetic prayer in the Christian church is not fortune-telling but Spirit-led encouragement that must be tested. Scripture commands, "Do not stifle the Holy Spirit. Do not scoff at prophecies, but test everything that is said. Hold on to what is good" (1 Thess 5:19–21, NLT). Believers are responsible to test every word by the Bible, retaining only what aligns with God's character and truth. Words that fail this test are discarded, because Scripture—not a prophet or prophecy, remains the final authority for the Christian life.

God's prophetic encouragement always reveals His character rather than creating dependence on a human figure. When Jesus spoke to the woman at the well, He revealed truths about her life that only God could know (John 4:29, NLT). This demonstration of divine knowledge brought her to repentance and faith, not bondage to a spiritual leader. In the same way, Christian prophecy is meant to draw believers to Christ, not to a person who claims special access to revelation.

Christian believers may receive many prophetic prayers throughout their lives. They are not restricted to a single blessing or a single person. These moments of prayer are invitations to partner with what God is doing, but their fulfillment depends not on human worthiness, fasting, or rituals, but on God's grace. The Word of God remains central, forming believers day by day through the transforming work of the Holy Spirit.

MORMONISM

In *Mormonism*, a patriarchal blessing is a once-in-a-lifetime pronouncement given by an ordained patriarch (fortune teller disguised as a spiritual prayer leader) within a local stake. This blessing is treated as a spiritual roadmap for the individual's life and often includes statements about lineage, future callings, personal missions, or divine expectations. The Book of Mormon teaches that God reveals specific futures to individuals through designated authorities (e.g., Alma 13:16; 3 Nephi 29:6), and the Doctrine and Covenants emphasizes the patriarch's role in giving inspired declarations that direct a person's life (D&C 124:91–92). In this prayer, like the movie Harry Potter, each member of the Mormon church will be placed in a lineage grouping, named by the 12 sons of Abraham.

Unlike Christian prophetic prayer, patriarchal blessings hold a fixed and authoritative role. They are typed, stored, and preserved in the Church's official records, functioning as a personal revelation that members are expected to study throughout life. Because these blessings are believed to define identity and destiny, many members cling to them even when circumstances change, viewing them as sacred promises linked to their faithfulness in the Mormon church.

This approach differs sharply from biblical teaching, which warns believers not to seek secret knowledge of the future or depend on human mediators for divine direction (Deut 18:10–12, NLT). In Scripture, God does not assign believers a tribal lineage that determines end-time roles, nor does He restrict revelation to a single spiritual moment. The New Testament centers all believers' identity in Christ alone, not in tribal affiliation or institutional authority.

Where the Bible teaches freedom in Christ and the continual guidance of the Holy Spirit, *Mormon* doctrine places lifelong spiritual dependence on a patriarchal blessing delivered by a single chosen officer. This system creates a fixed spiritual script for a person's life rather than the ongoing, relational transformation described in the New Testament. Christian prophetic encouragement must always be tested by Scripture, but patriarchal blessings function as authoritative personal revelation that members are expected to keep, study, and follow.

For Christians, the difference is clear: prophetic words are gifts that strengthen believers and always direct them back to the authority of the Bible. Their fulfillment rests in God's power, not in institutional hierarchy. In Christ, believers have continual access to God, receiving encouragement, correction, and direction through His Word and through the body of Christ—never through a single lifelong pronouncement that defines their destiny.

ANOINTING

In Scripture, anointing represents divine appointment and empowerment by the Holy Spirit. The Hebrew word māšîaḥ (מָשִׁיחַ) means "anointed one," from which we get Messiah. The Greek equivalent, Christos (Χριστός), means the same "Anointed One." Thus, Jesus Christ is the one and only Anointed One, chosen by God to redeem humanity (John 1:41, NLT).

In the Old Testament, prophets, priests, and kings were anointed as symbols of consecration for God's purpose (1 Samuel 16:13, NLT). Yet, these anointings only foreshadowed the ultimate and eternal anointing found in Jesus Christ. Hebrews teaches that Jesus is not one priest among many but the final and eternal High Priest, who entered once for all time into God's presence, offering His own blood for our salvation (Hebrews 9:11–12, NLT).

"Under the old system, the high priest entered the Most Holy Place only once a year… But Christ has now become the High Priest over all the good things that have come." (Hebrews 9:11, NLT)

Through His death and resurrection, Christ fulfilled all priestly duties and now mediates between God and humanity (1 Timothy 2:5, NLT). Believers are not called to become separate priests or kings through secret ceremonies, but rather, they share in Christ's anointing by the Holy Spirit when they place faith in Him.

"You have an anointing from the Holy One, and all of you know the truth." (1 John 2:20, NLT)

This anointing is not earned by works or temple rituals; it is the free gift of God through grace (Ephesians 2:8–9, NLT). Any attempt to claim divine power or priesthood apart from Christ's authority is contrary to Scripture, for Jesus said, "Apart from me you can do nothing" (John 15:5, NLT).

The true power of God's anointing produces fruit that glorifies Christ: healing, deliverance, love, and the transformation of lives (Acts 10:38, NLT). It is His Spirit, not human hierarchy, that confirms our identity as children of God and heirs with Christ (Romans 8:16–17, NLT).

MORMONISM

In contrast, *Mormonism* (LDS) teaches a secret temple ordinance known as the Second Anointing or Second Endowment. This practice, first introduced by Joseph Smith in the 1840s, is reserved for highly faithful members—often those in church leadership or long-term service. Participants are symbolically anointed as kings and queens, priests and priestesses, and are promised exaltation in the highest level of the Celestial Kingdom (Doctrine and Covenants 132:19–20; History of the Church, vol. 5).

This ordinance, though rarely mentioned publicly, is still quietly administered today to select couples in LDS temples. The seventh president, Heber J. Grant, significantly restricted its use in the early 20th century, but it has never been discontinued. According to LDS belief, the Second Anointing "seals one's exaltation", meaning those who receive it are assured of godhood and eternal life (Wikipedia, "Second Anointing," 2025).

This stands in direct contrast to the biblical teaching that only Christ's sacrifice ensures salvation. Scripture does not teach multiple tiers of exaltation, nor does it assign priesthood or divine status through secret ordinances. Instead, Jesus alone is called "King of kings and Lord of lords" (Revelation 19:16, NLT).

RACE

CHRISTIANITY

From Genesis to Revelation, Scripture consistently reveals that all people are created in the image of God and possess equal worth before Him. The Lord does not evaluate humanity based on physical appearance, skin color, or outward form but by the condition of the heart.

> "But the LORD said to Samuel, 'Don't judge by his appearance or height… The LORD doesn't see things the way you see them. People judge by outward appearance, but the LORD looks at the heart.'" (1 Samuel 16:7, NLT)

The Bible affirms that sin, not skin, separates humanity from God (Romans 3:23, NLT). Redemption, therefore, is a spiritual renewal, not a change in physical attributes. Isaiah illustrates this truth:

> "Though your sins are like scarlet, I will make them as white as snow." (Isaiah 1:18, NLT)

This verse speaks of spiritual cleansing, not literal skin color. Through Christ's blood, all people, regardless of ethnicity, are purified and reconciled to God (1 John 1:7, NLT).

Jesus Himself was not European, nor did He fit the idealized image often depicted in Western art. He was a first-century Jewish man of Middle Eastern descent. Isaiah described Him as having "no beauty or majesty that we should desire him" (Isaiah 53:2, NLT). His appearance was ordinary, emphasizing that salvation rests not on external form but on divine grace.

The New Testament church continued this inclusive message. Paul wrote,

> "There is no longer Jew or Gentile, slave or free, male and female. For you are all one in Christ Jesus." (Galatians 3:28, NLT)

At Pentecost, the Holy Spirit united believers from every nation and language (Acts 2:1–11, NLT). The gospel breaks racial, cultural, and social divisions because God's kingdom is beautifully diverse and unified in Christ.

The book of Revelation gives a picture of this final unity:

> "I saw a vast crowd, too great to count, from every nation and tribe and people and language, standing in front of the throne." (Revelation 7:9, NLT)

Biblical Christianity has never tied divine favor to skin tone or racial identity. God's masterpiece is humanity itself, made of many colors, languages, and nations, redeemed into one family through the Son of God (Ephesians 2:14–16, NLT).

MORMONISM

In contrast, *Mormon scripture* and history have tied skin color to divine favor and cursing. According to the Book of Mormon, dark skin was described as a visible mark of divine displeasure.

In 2 Nephi 5:21–23, the text states that God "caused a skin of blackness" to come upon the Lamanites so that they would "not be enticing" to the Nephites. This mark was said to pass to their children as a sign of separation. Alma 3:6–7 reinforces that their dark skin was a "mark" due to "transgression and rebellion." These passages directly associate righteousness with light skin and rebellion with dark skin.

Later verses, such as Mormon 9:6 and Jacob 3:8, describe spiritual purification as becoming "fair and white," language that implies lightness of skin is synonymous with righteousness. Historically, this teaching has influenced LDS racial perspectives and practices.

For over a century, Black men were barred from holding the priesthood or participating in temple ordinances, restrictions not lifted until 1978 (Doctrine and Covenants, Official Declaration 2). Although the LDS Church now disavows racial discrimination, these teachings remain in foundational texts that have not been revised.

Demographically, the LDS Church remains one of the least racially diverse major religions in the United States. Approximately 86% of its leadership is Caucasian, with a small percentage of Hispanic, Black, and Asian representation (Pew Research Center, 2025). Yet, official church media often portrays a more racially diverse image across platforms, creating a discrepancy between representation and reality (ex: African-American man on the front of their Ensign magazines).

This contrast between image and doctrine reveals an important theological difference: Biblical Christianity roots worth and purity in Christ's righteousness, while Mormon scripture historically connects divine favor to physical traits. The following biblical message proclaims equality in Christ; the LDS canon once portrayed spiritual hierarchy linked to race.

> "God does not show favoritism. In every nation he accepts those who fear him and do what is right." (Acts 10:34–35, NLT)

In light of Scripture, the belief that dark skin signifies a curse or divine disfavor is unbiblical. Christ's redemption does not alter pigmentation; it transforms hearts. The true mark of God's people is not skin tone but the indwelling of the Holy Spirit (Ephesians 1:13, NLT).

ORDINANCES

CHRISTIANITY

The Bible teaches that salvation is a gift of God, not a process of human ordinances or rituals. It is received through faith in Jesus Christ alone. Scripture declares,

> "God saved you by his grace when you believed. And you can't take credit for this; it is a gift from God. Salvation is not a reward for the good things we have done, so none of us can boast about it" (Ephesians 2:8–9, NLT).

Jesus Christ is the only Mediator between God and humanity:

> "For there is one God and one Mediator who can reconcile God and humanity, the man Christ Jesus" (1 Timothy 2:5, NLT).

Salvation does not come through religious acts, like in what we find in the Old Testament (Leviticus 1-15: burnt/sin/peace/grain offerings, dietary restrictions, ritual washings; Exodus 28-29 Priesthood Ordinations-see more in the chapter Dietary Laws) but through personal faith and repentance. The moment we trust in Christ's finished work on the cross, we are spiritually reborn:

> "If anyone belongs to Christ, he has become a new person. The old life is gone; a new life has begun!" (2 Corinthians 5:17, NLT).

When Jesus spoke to Nicodemus about being "born of water and the Spirit" (John 3:5), He was not teaching baptismal regeneration. He was describing two births, natural birth ("water") and spiritual birth ("Spirit"). Nicodemus misunderstood, thinking Jesus meant physical immersion, but Christ was pointing to the invisible transformation that happens when the Holy Spirit renews the heart (John 3:6–8).

Jesus' words on the cross, "It is finished" (John 19:30), marked the completion of salvation. Nothing can be added to it, not ceremonies, not priesthoods, and not temple rituals.

> "When he had cleansed us from our sins, he sat down in the place of honor at the right hand of the majestic God in heaven" (Hebrews 1:3, NLT).

Through faith alone, believers are sealed by the Holy Spirit and made children of God (Ephesians 1:13–14). This assurance is not earned by performance but secured by God's promise.

MORMONISM

In contrast, *Mormons* (LDS) teach that salvation and exaltation come through participation in specific ordinances. These are viewed as essential for eternal life and progression toward godhood.

1. Baptism by Immersion:

Mormons teach that baptism is required for the remission of sins and entrance into the kingdom of God (*Doctrine and Covenants 20:37*). They often cite John 3:5 to support this. However, this misinterprets Jesus' teaching, which referred to spiritual rebirth, not ritual cleansing.

2. Confirmation and the Gift of the Holy Ghost:

After baptism, members are confirmed by the laying on of hands to receive the Holy Ghost *(Articles of Faith 1:4)*.

3. The Sacrament (Communion):

The LDS sacrament is observed weekly to renew covenants made at baptism (*Moroni 4–5, Book of Mormon*).

4. Endowment Ceremony:

This temple ordinance imparts secret teachings and covenants believed necessary for exaltation (*Doctrine and Covenants 124:39*).

5. Temple Marriage (Sealing):

Mormons believe that marriages sealed in LDS temples continue for eternity (*Doctrine and Covenants 132:19–20*).

6. Priesthood Authority:

They teach that only men holding the Aaronic or Melchizedek priesthood can perform saving ordinances (*Doctrine and Covenants 84:19–22*).

7. Ordinances for the Dead:

Mormons perform baptisms and other rites on behalf of the dead, believing salvation can be offered to those who died without hearing the gospel *(Doctrine and Covenants 128:15–18)*.

These ordinances are seen as necessary steps toward exaltation, eternal life as gods and goddesses in the celestial kingdom.

(The Bible directly contradicts the notion that salvation depends on temple ordinances or priesthood authority.

"He himself is the sacrifice that atones for our sins—and not only our sins but the sins of all the world" (1 John 2:2, NLT).

God shows no favoritism (Romans 2:11). The invitation of salvation is open to all who believe, regardless of religious hierarchy or ritual observance.

"If you openly declare that Jesus is Lord and believe in your heart that God raised him from the dead, you will be saved" (Romans 10:9, NLT).

The Pharisees of Jesus' day clung to religious ordinances and traditions, yet Jesus rebuked them for missing the heart of faith. He fulfilled all righteousness on our behalf, freeing believers from the burden of ceremonial law (Matthew 5:17; Hebrews 10:10).

True salvation rests entirely on Christ's finished work, nothing more, and nothing less:

Hebrews 9:9-10 ASV, "Which is a figure for the time present, according to which are offered both gifts and sacrifices that cannot, as touching the conscience, make the worshipper perfect, being only (with meats and drinks and divers washings) carnal ordinances, imposed **UNTIL** a time of reformation.

The reformation has a name: JESUS.

THE BIBLICAL JESUS VS THE MORMON JESUS

CHRISTIANITY

The Bible presents Jesus as eternal God, not a created being nor a spirit child. "In the beginning the Word already existed… and the Word was God" (John 1:1, NLT). Jesus did not become divine; He has always been God. All creation came through Him: "God created everything through him… nothing was created except through him" (John 1:3, NLT). He is before all things and holds all things together, demonstrating His absolute divinity and authority (Col 1:16–17, NLT).

Scripture teaches that salvation is not earned but given through Christ's perfect righteousness. "Christ… never sinned… so that we could be made right with God" (2 Cor 5:21, NLT). His incarnation was a miraculous work of the Holy Spirit: "She was found to be pregnant through the Holy Spirit… the virgin will conceive a child" (Matt 1:18, 22–23, NLT). The biblical Jesus is God in the flesh, eternally one with the Father and the Spirit, for "the Lord our God is the one and only Lord" (Mark 12:29, NLT).

MORMONISM

Mormon LDS doctrine teaches a different Jesus. According to official teaching, Jesus is the firstborn spirit child of Heavenly Father and Heavenly Mother, the elder brother of all humanity, and even the brother of Lucifer *(Gospel Principles, 2011)*. His divinity is viewed as attained, and faithful Latter-day Saints may likewise progress to become gods, as promised in *Doctrine and Covenants 132:20.*

Mormonism also teaches that Jesus was physically begotten by an immortal Father rather than conceived solely by the Holy Spirit, contradicting the New Testament account. LDS scripture further separates the Father, Son, and Holy Ghost into three distinct gods united in purpose but not in essence (*D&C 130:22*).

The contrast continues in the character of Christ. The Book of Mormon depicts Jesus destroying cities and multitudes at His crucifixion (3 Nephi 8–10), while the biblical Jesus forgives His executioners and declares He came "not to destroy people's lives but to save them" (Luke 9:56, NLT).

Though both faiths call Him "Jesus," the identity, nature, and mission of Christ differ completely. The Jesus of Scripture is the eternal God and Savior. The Mormon Jesus is a created, exalted being within a hierarchy of gods. Only the true, biblical Christ holds the power to save.

DEAD SEA SCROLLS

One of the most important archaeological discoveries of the twentieth century occurred by the Dead Sea in 1947. A young shepherd tossing stones into a cave struck old clay jars and discovered ancient treasure hidden in the caves of Qumran. Between 1947 and 1956, scrolls and fragments from twelve caves were unearthed, now known as the Dead Sea Scrolls. More than nine hundred texts in Hebrew, Aramaic, and Greek were found, including every book of the Hebrew Bible except Esther and Nehemiah. The largest biblical scroll was an almost complete text of Isaiah.

The Dead Sea Scrolls are roughly one thousand years older than the previously known Hebrew manuscripts. When compared with the later Masoretic Text, scholars discovered that the scrolls matched with remarkable precision, over 95% identical, with only minor variations in spelling or style. This means the message of Scripture has been faithfully preserved through centuries of transmission. As the Bible declares, "The grass withers and the flowers fade, but the word of our God stands forever" (Isaiah 40:8, NLT). God's Word is reliable because He is faithful and unchanging: "Every word of God proves true" (Proverbs 30:5, NLT).

MORMONISM

Mormons teach that the Bible has not been perfectly transmitted. The Mormon *Eighth Article of Faith states: "We believe the Bible to be the word of God as far as it is translated correctly."* According to LDS teaching, many *"plain and precious truths"* were supposedly removed from the Bible over time, which led to the need for "restoration" through Joseph Smith and additional scriptures such as the Book of Mormon, Doctrine and Covenants, and Pearl of Great Price (Book of Mormon, *1 Nephi 13:28–29*).

Mormon leaders have interpreted Ezekiel 37:15–17, the "stick of Judah" and the "stick of Joseph", to mean the Bible and the Book of Mormon, claiming both are to be joined together as the Word of God. However, biblical context shows this passage refers to the future reunification of the divided tribes of Israel, not two separate books of scripture. Archaeology provides no evidence for the Book of Mormon's historical claims—no verified cities, languages, or artifacts have been found that support its narrative!

In contrast, the Dead Sea Scrolls strongly confirm the preservation of the Hebrew Scriptures. These findings undermine the LDS claim that the Bible has been corrupted. God has proven His Word to be consistent and reliable through both historical discovery and divine promise: "The words of the Lord are pure words, like silver tried in a furnace of earth, purified seven times. You, O Lord, will keep them; You will preserve them from this generation forever" (Psalm 12:6–7, NLT).

The discovery of the Dead Sea Scrolls stands as a monumental witness to the accuracy and faithfulness of Scripture. The Christian can stand confidently on the truth that God has preserved His Word without the need for additional revelation. The Bible remains complete, trustworthy, and divinely inspired, unchanging through centuries, just as the Author Himself is unchanging.

THE AUTHORITY OF SCRIPTURE

CHRISTIANITY

The Bible teaches that God's Word is complete, sufficient, and unchangeable. Scripture alone stands as the final authority for faith and practice.

Deuteronomy 4:2 warns, "Do not add to or subtract from these commands I am giving you. Just obey the commands of the Lord your God that I am giving you." (NLT). Similarly, Proverbs 30:6 cautions, "Do not add to his words, or he may rebuke you and expose you as a liar." The closing verses of Revelation echo the same command: "If anyone removes any of the words from this book of prophecy, God will remove that person's share in the tree of life" (Revelation 22:19, NLT).

These passages affirm that the Word of God is perfect and complete. To add or remove from it is to challenge God's authority. Christians believe that the Bible, inspired by the Holy Spirit, contains everything necessary for salvation and godly living (2 Timothy 3:16–17). No new revelation can supersede or amend what God has already spoken through His Word.

When sharing truth with others, including those in the Mormon faith, believers must remember that God's Word accomplishes His purposes. As Isaiah 55:10–11 (NLT) declares, "It is the same with my word. I send it out, and it always produces fruit. It will accomplish all I want it to, and it will prosper everywhere I send it."

This means Christians don't rely on persuasive arguments but on the living power of God's Word. When engaging those who believe differently, believers trust that Scripture itself has the authority and life to bring understanding and transformation.

In biblical Christianity, church leaders such as pastors and bishops are called to teach and preach God's Word faithfully (2 Timothy 4:2). The sermon is meant to explain Scripture clearly, exhort believers toward obedience, and protect the church from false teaching.

Christians hold firmly to Sola Scriptura, Scripture alone, as the guiding principle of faith. The Bible is not one of many sacred books but the singular revelation of God's truth.

MORMONISM

In *Mormonism*, authority does not rest solely on the Bible but on a collection of writings called the Standard Works, which include:

1. The Book of Mormon
2. Doctrine and Covenants (D&C)
3. The Pearl of Great Price
4. The Joseph Smith Translation (JST) of the Bible

Each of these texts contains teachings said to have been revealed through Joseph Smith or later prophets. The Doctrine and Covenants provides instructions about church organization, ordinances, and temple practices, including baptism for the dead and eternal marriage, concepts not found in the Bible.

The Pearl of Great Price includes Joseph Smith's retellings and additions to Genesis and Matthew, as well as the Book of Abraham, translated from Egyptian papyri.

These writings introduce doctrines such as the preexistence of human souls and exaltation to godhood.

The Joseph Smith Translation of the Bible claims to restore "lost truths" by altering, adding to, and reinterpreting passages of Scripture. This stands in direct opposition to biblical warnings against adding or removing from God's Word (Deuteronomy 4:2; Revelation 22:19).

Furthermore, LDS members believe in ongoing revelation through their living prophet, who speaks biannually at General Conference. His words are considered binding when approved by the church. In practice, this means new revelation can modify or expand previous doctrine, placing continual authority in human hands rather than in Scripture alone.

Mormon congregations differ from traditional Christian churches in structure and preaching. Each week, regular members, not ordained pastors, give "talks" rather than sermons. These messages are based on assigned topics and may include personal experience, opinion, or church materials such as *The Ensign* or *For the Strength of Youth*. The bishop presides but does not preach.

In contrast, biblical Christianity calls for trained shepherds to "preach the word; be prepared in season and out of season; correct, rebuke and encourage" (2 Timothy 4:2, NLT). The message must align with Scripture, not personal revelation or tradition.

Ultimately, while Mormonism embraces continuing revelation through modern prophets and additional scripture, Christianity teaches that God's revelation is complete in the Bible. Every new teaching must be tested against God's Word (1 John 4:1). If it does not align, it must be rejected. As believers, we rest in the sufficiency of Scripture and the unchanging truth of Christ.

DIETARY LAWS

CHRISTIANITY

Throughout Scripture, God reveals a progression from Old Testament ceremonial law to New Testament fulfillment in Christ. The dietary and ritual laws of the Old Covenant were given to Israel to set them apart as a holy nation (Leviticus 11). These practices, such as avoiding pork, shellfish, or eating only certain "clean" foods, were symbolic of spiritual purity and obedience to God.

However, these external restrictions pointed forward to something greater. Jesus Christ fulfilled the law, ending the need for ceremonial regulations and animal sacrifices. Hebrews 10:10–14 (NLT) teaches, "For God's will was for us to be made holy by the sacrifice of the body of Jesus Christ, once for all time." The law's purpose was to reveal sin and humanity's need for a Savior; Jesus became that perfect atonement.

Jesus Himself declared that food cannot make a person spiritually unclean. "Can't you see that the food you put into your body cannot defile you?… By saying this, he declared that every kind of food is acceptable in God's eyes" (Mark 7:18–19, NLT). The true defilement, He explained, comes not from what enters the mouth but from what comes out of the heart—evil thoughts, pride, and sin (Mark 7:20–21).

Peter's vision in Acts 10 confirmed that both Jews and Gentiles were no longer bound by the Mosaic food laws. God told Peter, "Do not call something unclean if God has made it clean" (Acts 10:15, NLT). The early church understood this as a divine shift: the gospel was for all nations, not just Israel, and food laws no longer separated people from God.

Paul further clarifies in Romans 14:14 (NLT), "I know and am convinced on the authority of the Lord Jesus that no food, in and of itself, is wrong to eat." In 1 Timothy 4:3–5 (NLT), he warns against false teachers who command abstinence from foods that God created "to be received with thanksgiving by those who know the truth."

Therefore, Christian freedom in eating and drinking is guided by gratitude and moderation, not restriction. "So whether you eat or drink, or whatever you do, do it all for the glory of God" (1 Corinthians 10:31, NLT).

Under the Old Covenant, the focus was on ritual obedience; under the New Covenant, the focus is on spiritual transformation through Christ. Believers are no longer bound by dietary codes because the law was fulfilled in Jesus. "For the law was given through Moses, but God's unfailing love and faithfulness came through Jesus Christ" (John 1:17, NLT).

MORMONISM

Mormons maintain a health code known as "*The Word of Wisdom*," recorded in *Doctrine and Covenants section 89*. According to this revelation, given to Joseph Smith in 1833, members are commanded to abstain from:

- Alcohol ("strong drink"),
- Tobacco,
- Hot drinks (interpreted by LDS leaders as coffee and tea), and
- Illegal or harmful substances.

The text also promotes the use of grains, fruits, and herbs, and recommends that meat be eaten sparingly (*Doctrine and Covenants 89:10–17*). Adherence to the Word of Wisdom is considered a commandment, and observance is required for full participation in temple worship.

This contrasts with the biblical understanding of food and freedom. In the New Testament, dietary restrictions were fulfilled in Christ and no longer serve as measures of righteousness or worthiness before God. In Mormonism, however, obedience to the Word of Wisdom functions as a modern law of health and worthiness, similar to how Mosaic food laws once distinguished the Israelites.

The LDS Guide to the Scriptures states that the Word of Wisdom *"is a law of health and obedience given by revelation,"* and keeping it "brings both physical and spiritual blessings." In this system, abstaining from certain drinks or foods becomes a mark of spiritual commitment and covenant faithfulness.

Yet Scripture warns against elevating human rules to divine authority. Paul writes, "You have died with Christ, and he has set you free from the spiritual powers of this world. So why do you keep on following the rules of the world, such as 'Don't handle! Don't taste! Don't touch!'?" (Colossians 2:20–21, NLT). Such regulations, he explains, "may seem wise because they require strong devotion… but they provide no help in conquering a person's evil desires" (Colossians 2:23, NLT).

While healthy living and self-control are virtues, they are not requirements for salvation or spiritual purity. In Christianity, righteousness comes through faith in Jesus Christ, not dietary observance (Romans 3:22).Believers are called to test every teaching against Scripture (1 John 4:1). The Word of God stands complete and final, no new revelation or dietary rule can improve upon the freedom Christ secured on the cross.

DECISIONS

CHRISTIANITY

In Christianity, decisions are important, yet they do not determine your eternal destiny or the measure of God's love for you. Scripture shows that God, not human choices, ultimately governs the course of life. The rain falls on both the righteous and the wicked (Matthew 5:45, NLT), illustrating God's common grace, meaning he sustains life for all people regardless of their moral standing. Likewise, hardships are not punishments for mistakes but part of God's sovereign plan.

Decisions still matter, they reflect obedience, faith, and stewardship, but they do not bind God's love or determine ultimate outcomes. Christian teaching emphasizes trusting God's guidance and acknowledging that while we exercise discernment, our future rests in His hands (Proverbs 3:5–6, NLT). Hardships, trials, or natural disasters are not moral judgments on our choices; they are opportunities for God's glory to be revealed and for His purposes to be fulfilled (Romans 8:28, NLT). Believers are invited to act responsibly and wisely, yet with the assurance that God's grace is constant, unearned, and unconditional. In the words of Jesus in John 15:16 NLT, "You didn't choose me. I chose you. I appointed you to go and produce lasting fruit, so that the Father will give you whatever you ask for in my name."

MORMONISM

In contrast, *Mormon* teachings place significant weight on human decisions in shaping both temporal and eternal outcomes. The concept of "Choose the Right" (CTR) emphasizes that every choice can impact your salvation and future blessings. "CTR" rings are sold worldwide from LDS stores. The Mormon hymn "Choose The Right" is sung frequently in LDS churches:

"...Choose the right when a choice is placed before you, in the right the Holy Spirit guides..."

This song emphasizes the Holy Spirit being that conscience angel on your shoulder. Let us remember that "sin" in Mormonism can include: Drinking Coffee and Tea.

LDS sources teach that consistently choosing rightly leads to a straighter path, while poor choices can result in hardship or spiritual disadvantage like the Holy Spirit leaving you. The cultural emphasis often extends to health, family planning, and daily conduct, suggesting that difficulties are frequently consequences of personal choices (The Church of Jesus Christ of Latter-day Saints, 1995).

While the scriptures of the LDS tradition, including the Book of Mormon and Doctrine and Covenants, recognize divine providence, the broader cultural interpretation often links misfortune to human error. Illness, financial struggles, or other hardships may be perceived as a result of choices, in contrast to the biblical view that suffering occurs independent of individual guilt and that God's purposes transcend our understanding.

CALLED AND CHOSEN

CHRISTIANITY

Jesus taught, "For many are called, but few are chosen" (Matthew 22:14, NLT). This distinction reveals the difference between general invitation and divine election.

God's call extends broadly, through the gospel, all are invited to come to Him. Yet being chosen refers to those who respond in faith and are made new in Christ. Believers are not chosen for their works or worthiness but because of God's sovereign grace. "You didn't choose me. I chose you. I appointed you to go and produce lasting fruit" (John 15:16, NLT).

Being chosen means belonging to God in covenant relationship, washed, redeemed, and set apart. "For God so loved the world that he gave his one and only Son, so that everyone who believes in him will not perish but have eternal life" (John 3:16, NLT). Through Christ's sacrifice, we are not only called but also adopted as children of God (Ephesians 1:4–5, NLT).

The chosen walk by faith, allowing God to reveal which works bear fruit and which do not. They live in dependence upon His Spirit, not waiting for new directions but moving in obedience to the truth already revealed in His Word. "God is working in you, giving you the desire and the power to do what pleases him" (Philippians 2:13, NLT).

To be chosen is to be claimed by God Himself: "Do not be afraid, for I have ransomed you. I have called you by name; you are mine" (Isaiah 43:1, NLT). This is not a temporary calling but an eternal relationship, grounded in Christ's finished work.

Those who are chosen reflect the Father's nature, for a good tree cannot bear bad fruit (Matthew 7:17–18, NLT). The fruit of a chosen life is the visible evidence of inward transformation, rooted in grace, not human effort.

In biblical theology, being called refers to God's universal invitation to salvation. Being chosen describes the believer's identity and purpose within that salvation, secured by God's <u>initiative</u>, not man's ambition.

MORMONISM

In *Mormonism,* the concepts of being "called" and "chosen" appear in *Doctrine and Covenants 121:34–36:*

"Behold, there are many called, but few are chosen. And why are they not chosen? Because their hearts are set so much upon the things of this world, and aspire to the honors of men..."

Here, "being chosen" is tied to worthiness and the proper exercise of priesthood authority. The passage continues, teaching that those who misuse their callings lose God's power. In this system, a person's "calling" is often tied to a Church assignment, priesthood office, or missionary duty, and "being chosen" refers to proving oneself faithful in those responsibilities.

This interpretation differs significantly from the biblical meaning. In Mormon doctrine, callings are positions to fulfill, often seen as steps in one's spiritual progression. Once a calling ends, another is sought.

Salvation and exaltation are closely connected to obedience, ordinances, and temple worthiness.

The <u>LDS Guide to the Scriptures</u> defines *"Calling and Election"* as a process where a person's exaltation is made sure through continued righteousness and covenant faithfulness. The LDS member must be married in an LDS temple to gain this highest kingdom. This idea extends salvation into a system of performance and progression, rather than a finished act of redemption through Jesus Christ.

In contrast, BIBLICAL Scripture teaches that God's calling and choosing are final and secure: "For God's gifts and his call can never be withdrawn" (Romans 11:29, NLT). The chosen are not maintained by their faithfulness to tasks but by Christ's faithfulness to His covenant.

One system depends on human progression; the other rests on divine election. In Christ, being chosen means being His forever, forgiven, sealed, and empowered to bear good fruit that glorifies the Father.

PRAISE

CHRISTIANITY

Praise is the natural response of a heart that knows the gospel. In Scripture, God invites His people to proclaim His goodness openly: "I will praise the Lord at all times. I will constantly speak His praises" (Ps. 34:1, NLT). Praise is not silent or passive; it flows from gratitude for God's grace, His presence, and His provision.

Jesus teaches that God Himself supplies every need of His children, and believers glorify Him by depending on Him: "You can ask for anything in my name, and I will do it" (John 14:13, NLT). This dependence can look strange to the world. Christians appear humble, even weak, because they willingly surrender their own will and strength to God. Yet this surrender is what fills them daily with the Spirit's supernatural love (Gal. 5:22–23, NLT). Their lives become a testimony: every answered prayer becomes another reason to praise.

Jesus told Nicodemus that unless a person is born again, they cannot "see the Kingdom of God" (John 3:3, NLT). Praise comes from this new birth, eyes opened to God's goodness, hearts awakened to His grace. Christians praise because they truly know the Good News. They know the One who saved them, loves them, and lives within them. Praise is the overflow of a redeemed heart.

MORMONISM

In the Mormon Church of Jesus Christ of Latter-day Saints, worship is primarily expressed through reverence, quietness, restraint, and orderly behavior. LDS manuals and culture emphasize folded arms, silence, and subdued posture as the proper way to show respect in worship settings. Praise, in the biblical sense of joyful proclamation, is not central to LDS practice or theology.

This difference flows from doctrine. LDS teaching does not present salvation as the finished work of Christ applied by grace alone. Instead, members progress toward exaltation through ordinances, covenants, and continued worthiness (Doctrine and Covenants 82:10; 1 Nephi 3:7). Because their standing with God depends on sustained obedience and personal righteousness, the focus is on duty rather than celebration. Their "good news" is not the completed gospel of Scripture but a system they must continually uphold.

The Book of Mormon and Doctrine and Covenants teach that exaltation requires personal perfection, covenant keeping, and faithfulness to LDS ordinances (*2 Nephi 25:23; Doctrine and Covenants 132*). In such a system, assurance is conditional and ongoing. Praise in the biblical sense, overflowing joy in Christ's finished work, is naturally absent because the work is not considered finished.

2 Nephi 29:9 "...for my work is not yet finished; neither shall it be *until the end of man, neither from that time henceforth and forever."*

In contrast, Christians praise because the gospel is complete. Jesus has already done what we could never do. Praise rises where grace is understood, where salvation is secure, and where the heart knows the freedom of the true Good News.

FLESH

CHRISTIANITY

When Jesus read from Isaiah in His hometown synagogue, declaring prophecy fulfilled, the people rejected Him (Luke 4:18–24, NLT). Their hearts were hardened, they wanted to throw him off a cliff because the flesh resists truth.

"The sinful nature wants to do evil, which is just the opposite of what the Spirit wants." (Galatians 5:17, NLT)
"Those who are still under the control of their sinful nature can never please God." (Romans 8:8, NLT)

The flesh seeks comfort, not conviction. Yet Jesus calls His followers to deny themselves:

"If any of you wants to be my follower, you must give up your own way, take up your cross, and follow me." (Matthew 16:24, NLT)

The Holy Spirit does not confirm truth through feelings but through the Word of God.

"Man shall not live by bread alone, but by every word that comes from the mouth of God." (Matthew 4:4, NLT)

Our emotions can mislead us, but God's Word is steady and unchanging:

"The heart is deceitful above all things, and desperately wicked." (Jeremiah 17:9, NLT)

Salvation is not achieved by perfecting the flesh, but by crucifying it.

"Those who belong to Christ Jesus have nailed the passions and desires of their sinful nature to his cross and crucified them there." (Galatians 5:24, NLT)

The Christian's assurance comes from Scripture and the indwelling Spirit, not from subjective impressions.

"For God is working in you, giving you the desire and the power to do what pleases him." (Philippians 2:13, NLT)

MORMONISM

In *Mormonism, Doctrine and Covenants 9:8–9*, Joseph Smith taught with the intention of directing members to read the Book of Mormon:

"You must study it out in your mind; then you must ask me if it be right… if it is right I will cause that your bosom shall burn within you… But if it be not right you shall have a stupor of thought that shall cause you to forget the thing which is wrong."

This teaching suggests truth is confirmed by physical or emotional sensation. Yet Scripture warns that the human heart and feelings cannot be trusted apart from God's revealed Word (Jeremiah 17:9).

In LDS practice, members are encouraged to discern truth through such feelings, what is often called a "burning in the bosom." But the Bible teaches discernment comes through testing all things by Scripture:

"Test everything that is said. Hold on to what is good."
(1 Thessalonians 5:21, NLT)
"Your word is a lamp to guide my feet and a light for my path." (Psalm 119:105, NLT)

The danger of relying on feeling-based confirmation is that the flesh can imitate the Spirit. True believers are called to walk by faith in God's Word, not by emotional response.

Thus, Mormonism locates truth in sensation; Christianity locates truth in revelation. One follows feeling; the other follows faith.

HELL

Biblical scripture presents hell as a real, eternal place of judgment, created for the devil and his angels but also the final destination for all who reject Christ. Jesus describes it with sobering clarity: "Depart from me…into the eternal fire prepared for the devil and his angels" (Matthew 25:41, NLT). Hell is not symbolic. It is conscious separation from God, described as torment, darkness, fire, and unending loss.

Jesus' account of the rich man and Lazarus gives one of the clearest pictures. The rich man, having ignored God in life, lifted his eyes in torment immediately after death and begged for relief: "I am in anguish in these flames" (Luke 16:24, NLT). His suffering was real, immediate, and irreversible. He longed to warn his family, but he was told that those who will not believe God's Word now will not believe even if someone rises from the dead (Luke 16:31, NLT). There is no second chance beyond the grave. Scripture affirms that "each person is destined to die once and after that comes judgment" (Hebrews 9:27, NLT).

1 Corinthians 1:18 "For the message of the cross is foolishness to those who are perishing, but to us who are being saved it is the power of God."
The Greek verb "perishing" in Strong's interlinear concordance (G575) is "1. To destroy (A to put out of the

way entirely, abolish, put an end to ruin; B render useless; C to kill; D to declare that one must be put to death E. Metaphor. To devote or give over to eternal misery in hell F. To perish, to be lost, ruined, destroyed."

Hell is self-chosen in its rejection of Christ, yet divinely appointed in justice. It is eternal separation from God, and Jesus Himself is the One who finally separates the sheep from the goats (Matthew 25:32–33, NLT). Scripture never softens this reality. Its purpose is not to frighten but to sober the heart and lead us to Christ, who alone saves from judgment and brings us into eternal life.

MORMONISM

Mormon Latter-day Saint doctrine presents a very different view of hell. In Mormon theology, "Spirit Prison" is usually temporary and functions more like a place of purification. Most individuals, including those who rejected Christ in this life, are taught that they will receive additional opportunities after death to accept the LDS gospel through spirit-world missionary work *(Doctrine and Covenants 138)*. After this process, nearly everyone eventually inherits one of three kingdoms of glory. Thus, "hell" for the vast majority is neither eternal nor final.

Mormonism's only permanent hell is "outer darkness," reserved for a small, elite group called "sons of perdition"—those who were LDS, received full knowledge, and then deliberately rejected it (*Doctrine and Covenants 76*). This is not the biblical teaching. Scripture presents no hierarchy of heavens, no prolonged progression after death, and no additional chances to repent. Instead, Jesus teaches one final division: those who belong to Him and those who do not.

The LDS model reframes hell as a fourth kingdom and makes eternal judgment rare. The Bible makes hell the sober, certain outcome for all who reject Christ's salvation. The LDS model promises postmortem progression; the Bible teaches finality. The LDS model defines hell in relation to Mormon covenants; the Bible defines it in relation to Christ alone.

Christian theology is consistent, clear, and urgent: judgment is final, hell is real, and Christ is the only escape. Mormon theology softens the warning and extends hope where Scripture does not. One message draws the heart to repentance today; the other offers chances tomorrow that God has never promised. Scripture's call stands: "Today…hear his voice" (Hebrews 3:15, NLT).

SUFFERING

CHRISTIANITY

Jesus warned His followers that suffering would accompany true discipleship:

"Blessed are you when people mock you and persecute you and lie about you and say all sorts of evil things against you because you are my followers." (Matthew 5:11, NLT)
"If the world hates you, remember that it hated me first." (John 15:18, NLT)

To suffer for Christ's name is to share in His mission and His victory. The Apostle Paul said,

"For I will show him how much he must suffer for my name's sake." (Acts 9:16, NLT)

Such suffering refines faith and reveals belonging to God's family.

"For God called you to do good, even if it means suffering… Christ suffered for you. He is your example." (1 Peter 2:21, NLT)

True believers endure rejection not for self-righteous causes but for righteousness itself.

"If you are insulted because you bear the name of Christ, you will be blessed." (1 Peter 4:14, NLT)

Those who belong to Christ choose to suffer with God's people rather than enjoy temporary comfort:

"He chose to share the oppression of God's people instead of enjoying the fleeting pleasures of sin." (Hebrews 11:25, NLT)

Jesus calls believers to love even those who oppose them:

"Love your enemies! Do good to those who hate you. Bless those who curse you. Pray for those who hurt you." (Luke 6:27–28, NLT)

When we suffer for His name's sake, we reflect His love and share in His life.

"For to you it has been granted for Christ's sake not only to believe in Him but also to suffer for Him." (Philippians 1:29, NLT)

This suffering is not punishment but participation, proof of belonging to the one true Savior.

"He who loses his life for my sake will find it." (Matthew 10:39, NLT)

MORMONISM

In *Mormonism* doctrine, suffering is often seen as a process of proving personal righteousness. Joseph Smith taught that obedience to commandments and enduring trials earn divine exaltation. *Doctrine and Covenants 121:7–8 records,*

"My son, peace be unto thy soul; thine adversity and thine afflictions shall be but a small moment... if thou endure it well, God shall exalt thee on high."

This view ties suffering to progression and reward, implying that endurance elevates one toward godhood (Doctrine and Covenants 132:20). Salvation, then, becomes a path of earning eternal life through personal worthiness and covenant keeping.

By contrast, Scripture teaches that suffering for Christ is not a means to personal exaltation but a mark of identification with Him. It is God's grace, not man's endurance, that saves and sustains.

> "God saved you by his grace when you believed. And you can't take credit for this; it is a gift from God." (Ephesians 2:8, NLT)

Mormonism frames suffering as a necessary step in human exaltation. Christianity sees it as fellowship with the crucified Christ. The first exalts man's effort; the second glorifies God's mercy.

ATONEMENT

The Bible teaches that the atonement was accomplished on the cross, not in the Garden of Gethsemane. Luke describes Jesus' agony in the garden with a simile, not literal bleeding: His sweat "fell to the ground like great drops of blood" (Luke 22:44, NLT). His suffering there prepared Him for the real sacrifice to come, the shedding of His blood on the cross.

Only a perfect, sinless Savior could deal with humanity's sin. The Bible teaches that sin entered the world through Adam, and because of that, every person is born with a sinful nature:

- "Everyone has sinned" (Romans 3:23, NLT).
- "I was born a sinner" (Psalm 51:5, NLT).
- "When Adam sinned, sin entered the world" (Romans 5:12, NLT).

This is why Christ came as the Last Adam, the only One able to reverse the curse:

"The first Adam became a living person… the last Adam, Christ, is a life-giving Spirit" (1 Corinthians 15:45, NLT).

The work was fully completed at the cross. Jesus declared, "It is finished!" (John 19:30, NLT). Through His blood we receive redemption and forgiveness:

- "He purchased our freedom with the blood of his Son" (Ephesians 1:7, NLT).

- "Through this man Jesus there is forgiveness for your sins" (Acts 13:38, NLT).
- "God made Christ, who never sinned, to be the offering for our sin" (2 Corinthians 5:21, NLT).

The cross is the center of Christian faith because it is the place where sin was paid for, the curse was overturned, and grace was secured. Without the cross, there is no redemption. With the cross, the work is complete.

MORMONISM

Official *Mormon LDS* doctrine presents a different understanding of the atonement. In Mormonism, the atonement took place primarily in the Garden of Gethsemane, where Jesus is said to have suffered for sin and "bled from every pore" (Doctrine and Covenants 19:18; Mosiah 3:7). The cross is important, but it is not the center of the atoning work. There are pictures of European Jesus kneeling at the Garden of Gethsemane all over their church buildings.

LDS teaching also rejects the biblical doctrine of inherited sin. According to *Article of Faith #2, "Men will be punished for their own sins, and not for Adam's transgression."* Because of this, Mormon doctrine views Adam's fall as a necessary step of progression, not as the event that corrupted all humanity.

These two beliefs shape LDS doctrine of the atonement:

1. Location of the Atonement

- LDS: The atonement occurred in Gethsemane through suffering and spiritual anguish.
- Bible: The atonement occurred on the cross through the shedding of Jesus's blood.

2. Nature of Sin

- LDS: Humans are not born sinners; sin is personal wrongdoing.
- Bible: Humanity inherits a sinful nature and stands under Adam's fall.

Because Mormonism does not see humanity as fallen in Adam, the atonement becomes a way to empower people to return to God through obedience, ordinances, and covenants. It is not a once-for-all substitution, but a step in a larger system of personal progression.

FORGIVENESS AND RESTORATION

CHRISTIANITY

God often brings us back to painful moments, not to shame us, but to heal us. When we ask, "Lord, what are You teaching me?" We invite His Spirit to do the deep work. Scripture says, "People do not live by bread alone, but by every word that comes from the mouth of God" (Matthew 4:4, NLT).

True forgiveness releases both us and the offender. Jesus commanded, "Love your enemies! Pray for those who persecute you!" (Matthew 5:44, NLT). When we forgive, we are no longer bound by bitterness; we make space for God to restore.

Confrontation, when led by the Spirit, is an act of love. Jesus taught, "If another believer sins against you, go privately and point out the offense… If the person listens and confesses it, you have won that person back" (Matthew 18:15, NLT). The goal is always reconciliation, not revenge.

God reminds us, "No weapon turned against you will succeed" (Isaiah 54:17, NLT). Our security rests in His righteousness, not our control. Forgiveness doesn't mean approving of sin; it means entrusting judgment to the Lord who sees all.

When God forgives, it's a done deal. "IT IS FINISHED" were his words (John 19:30).

MORMONISM

Mormonism teaches that forgiveness and grace are conditional, earned through effort. *The Book of Mormon reads, "It is by grace that we are saved, after all we can do" (2 Nephi 25:23)*. This view contrasts sharply with Scripture, which declares, "God saved you by his grace when you believed. And you can't take credit for this; it is a gift from God" (Ephesians 2:8, NLT).

Joseph Smith also taught, *"If what you feel is right, it is right, and if it is not right, you will forget the thought" (Teachings of the Prophet Joseph Smith, p. 151)*. But the Bible warns, "The heart is deceitful above all things" (Jeremiah 17:9, NLT). Forgiveness and truth do not come from feelings—they come from the unchanging Word of God.

In Mormonism, people strive to earn worthiness; in Christ, forgiveness is freely given. "If we confess our sins, he is faithful and just to forgive us our sins and to cleanse us from all wickedness" (1 John 1:9, NLT).

HEAVEN

Heaven, according to Scripture, is not a place of hierarchy or human advancement, it is the eternal dwelling place of God and His redeemed people. The Lord declares, "Heaven is my throne, and the earth is my footstool. Could you build me a temple as good as that?" (Isaiah 66:1, NLT). God does not dwell in temples made by hands but in the hearts of those who are humble and contrite before Him (Isaiah 66:2, NLT).

The Bible teaches that believers will dwell eternally with Jesus Christ in the new heaven and new earth. "Look! God's home is now among his people! He will live with them, and they will be his people. God himself will be with them" (Revelation 21:3, NLT). Heaven is described not by levels or classes, but by perfect communion with God, where "there will be no more death or sorrow or crying or pain" (Revelation 21:4, NLT).

The apostle Paul explained that while there are different types of created bodies, earthly and heavenly (1 Corinthians 15:40, NLT), he was not describing separate heavens of human progression but contrasting the natural body with the resurrected, spiritual one (1 Corinthians 15:44, NLT).

Our eternal hope is grounded in grace, not in temple ordinances or progression. Jesus declared, "It is finished!" (John 19:30, NLT). The redemptive work required for eternal life is complete. Those who believe in Him are promised everlasting life, "for God so loved the

world that he gave his one and only Son" (John 3:16,
NLT).

Heaven is not built by man, nor purchased by
works, but prepared by Christ Himself: "There is more
than enough room in my Father's home… I am going to
prepare a place for you" (John 14:2, NLT).

MORMONISM

Mormon doctrine teaches a three-tiered heaven: the
celestial, terrestrial, and telestial kingdoms, revealed to
Joseph Smith in *Doctrine and Covenants 76*. The celestial
kingdom is described as the highest glory, where God and
the most faithful dwell, including those married and sealed
in Mormon temples.

The Book of Mormon references, "There are also
celestial bodies, and bodies terrestrial" (1 Corinthians
15:40, KJV), but in LDS theology, this verse is expanded
into a structure of eternal progression between kingdoms.
Mormonism teaches that exalted individuals can
eventually become gods themselves (*Doctrine and
Covenants 132:20*).

In LDS temples, the "celestial room" symbolizes
this exalted state, filled with light, gold, and white
furnishings meant to represent divine glory. It reflects the
belief that faithful members can dwell with God after
proving worthiness through ordinances, marriage
covenants, and obedience to Church law.

However, Scripture refutes the notion of human
exaltation or tiered heavens. The Lord alone is God:
"Before me there was no God formed, neither shall there
be after me" (Isaiah 43:10, NLT). Eternal life is a gift, not
a promotion.

Mormon doctrine also teaches continued missionary work in the afterlife among lower kingdoms, a concept not supported in the Bible. Instead, Scripture affirms that judgment follows death: "Each person is destined to die once and after that comes judgment" (Hebrews 9:27, NLT).

The Bible reveals only one eternal destiny for the redeemed, dwelling in the presence of Christ forever. There are no higher or lower glories for the saved, only the perfect unity of the body of Christ (Revelation 21:22–23, NLT).

WORSHIP

Worship means worth-ship (got this from my Bishop Hooks!), giving worth to the One who is truly worthy. We worship God not only for what He has done but for who He is. Praise celebrates His actions; worship honors His nature.

True worship begins in faith, before we see results. Like King Jehoshaphat, we worship while trusting that God will act. When Judah faced a vast army, Jehoshaphat prayed, "We do not know what to do, but we are looking to you for help" (2 Chronicles 20:12, NLT). God responded, "Do not be afraid or discouraged… for the battle is not yours, but God's" (v.15). As the people WORSHIPED, God gave them victory and joy (vv.18–27).

Worship is obedience and surrender. It's lifting our eyes from fear and focusing on His eternal worth. "For God is Spirit, so those who worship him must worship in spirit and in truth" (John 4:24, NLT).

Forgiveness flows out of true worship. When we realize how much we've been forgiven, our hearts bow in humility and gratitude. "If you forgive those who sin against you, your heavenly Father will forgive you" (Matthew 6:14, NLT). Worship isn't just songs, it's a life that honors the mercy we've received.

We were created to worship (Isaiah 43:21). Everything else fades: wealth, status, temples, and even our bodies, but "the word of our God stands forever" (Isaiah 40:8, NLT). Therefore, our worship must center on Him alone, not on anything made by human hands or imagination.

MORMONISM

Mormon doctrine often blends worship with human effort, ritual, and hierarchy. Temples, ordinances, and worthiness interviews are emphasized as ways to draw near to God. <u>The Guide to the Scriptures</u> defines worship as including "prayer, fasting, service, and temple attendance" acts that imply human participation earns closeness with God.

Thus, while the Bible calls us to worship God for who He is and trust His finished work, Mormonism ties worship to human worthiness and ritual performance, shifting the focus from the worthiness of Christ to the efforts of man.

THE WORLD

Scripture uses the term "the world" to describe humanity in its fallen state, people who remain in sin, apart from Christ, and still under self-condemnation. It does not mark a religious group but the spiritual condition of anyone who has not yet received salvation. John writes, "But you belong to God, my dear children. You have already won a victory over those people, because the Spirit who lives in you is greater than the spirit who lives in the world" (1 John 4:4, NLT). The distinction is spiritual, not institutional.

The Word of God cuts through every human barrier. Scripture is living and active, able to pierce through culture, language, disease, and circumstance. In the early church, Jews and Gentiles were divided by deep cultural and religious boundaries, including circumcision and concepts of purity, but the cross brought both to the same place: sinners in need of a Savior. God's ways rise higher than human categories or systems. As Isaiah declares, "My thoughts are nothing like your thoughts… And my ways are far beyond anything you could imagine" (Isaiah 55:8–9, NLT). In this truth, we learn that we are spiritual beings living a human life, called into unity by Christ alone.

MORMONISM

Mormon Latter-day Saint teaching often interprets "the world" as those outside the LDS Church, individuals who have not accepted Mormonism and therefore remain under the influence of *"worldliness"*. This institutional category shapes identity and belonging, framing "the world" as all who are <u>not faithful members of the restored mormon church</u>. Official *LDS* teachings frequently present a contrast between members and non-members, emphasizing that safety, revelation, and spiritual victory are found within the covenant structure of the Church rather than in the universal body of Christ.

This stands in contrast to Scripture's definition. The Bible never equates "the world" with a specific organization or denomination but with the fallen human condition itself. According to biblical teaching, the dividing line is not between Mormon and non-Mormon, but between belief and unbelief, repentance and rebellion, salvation and spiritual darkness.

HOLY SPIRIT

CHRISTIANITY

The Bible presents the Holy Spirit as the very presence of God: eternal, personal, powerful, and inseparable from the Father and the Son. Jesus promised that the Spirit would live with believers and dwell within them, not as a visiting influence but as God Himself taking up residence in His people (John 14:16–17, NLT). The Spirit is the Comforter who remains forever, guiding believers into truth, strengthening them for spiritual warfare, and revealing God's love in ways that transform the heart without relying on fragile emotional signals.

Throughout Scripture, God directs His people to test everything and cling to what is true (1 Thess. 5:21, NLT). Human feelings are unreliable indicators of truth, and Jesus repeatedly warned that the human heart can be misled. Emotions rise and fall, and even strong sensations, whether tears, warmth, or excitement, can come from sources entirely unrelated to God. The Holy Spirit instead reveals truth through Scripture, godly wisdom, conviction, and the fruit He produces in a believer's life. He equips the church with diverse spiritual gifts, all meant to serve and strengthen the body of Christ (1 Cor. 12:4–7, NLT). His voice pierces the soul not with condemnation, but with clarity and love, because "there is no condemnation for those who belong to Christ Jesus" (Rom. 8:1, NLT).

God never silences honest questions. The Christian life is built on truth, not suppression. The Lord welcomes seekers and leads them through Scripture, counsel, and wisdom. When believers wrestle with doubt, God provides solid answers rather than urging them to ignore their concerns. His Spirit reassures, convicts, comforts, and illuminates, always pointing them back to the Word.

MORMONISM

Mormon doctrine teaches that truth is confirmed primarily through emotion, especially warmth, tingling, or the *"burning in the bosom." Moroni 10:4–5* instructs members that if they ask God *"with a sincere heart, with real intent,"* He will manifest truth through the Holy Ghost, which is widely interpreted as an emotional sensation. Joseph Smith likewise described a *"burning in my bosom"* as a sign of spiritual truth (*Joseph Smith History 1:20*). Generations of Latter-day Saints have been taught that tears, shivers, and swelling emotions indicate the Spirit's presence.

However, these sensations are biologically normal responses produced by the autonomic nervous system. They can be triggered by music, films, nostalgia, fear, or memory just as easily as by spiritual reflection. This places enormous weight on a person's inward feelings and equates temporary sensations with divine revelation. When emotional experiences become the foundation of spiritual certainty, members often interpret ordinary physiological reactions as sacred confirmation.

Latter-day Saint culture reinforces this by encouraging members to *"doubt your doubts before you doubt your faith,"* a phrase used by President Russell M. Nelson. This motto discourages genuine examination, even though Scripture calls believers to examine everything in the light of God's truth. The biblical model invites honest evaluation; LDS teaching often urges emotional loyalty.

Mormon doctrine also presents the Holy Ghost as a separate God—unembodied, waiting for eventual exaltation, and distinct from both the Father and the Son. Some LDS teachers have even suggested that the Holy Ghost may someday receive a body or marry. This sharply diverges from Scripture, which teaches that the Holy Spirit is fully God, eternally divine, and not a being in process.

The *LDS* emphasis on a *"still small voice,"* interpreted largely through feelings, places spiritual discernment on subjective impression rather than biblical revelation.

The biblical message is firm: the Holy Spirit is God Himself, not a separate deity, not a spirit awaiting progression, and not a fleeting presence dependent on human performance. He comforts believers, brings Scripture to remembrance, and guides them into truth that is anchored in God's unchanging Word. The Christian faith rests on the reliability of God's revelation, not the unpredictability of human emotion.

Biblical Christianity is grounded in truth, not tingles.

ESCHATOLOGY

Jesus Christ will return as the victorious King. Revelation 19:11–16 (NLT) describes His second coming: "Then I saw heaven opened, and a white horse was standing there. Its rider was named Faithful and True… He wore a robe dipped in blood, and His title was King of all kings and Lord of all lords." From His mouth comes a sharp sword, His Word, by which He conquers evil.

Before this final return, Scripture reveals a period called the Tribulation (Revelation 6). It will last seven years, divided into two halves, the second more severe than the first (Daniel 9:27). Yet believers in Christ are promised deliverance from this wrath: "For God chose to save us through our Lord Jesus Christ… so we can live with Him forever" (1 Thessalonians 5:9–10, NLT).

Revelation 2–3 contains messages to seven churches, each teaching believers how to remain faithful. Jesus commends love, endurance, and truth but warns against hypocrisy, false teaching, and lukewarm faith. He calls His people to repent and return to their first love, Himself (Revelation 2:4–5).

As the seals are opened in Revelation 6, the world witnesses famine, war, and death, symbolized by the Four Horsemen. Yet through it all, God remains sovereign, and Christ's return will establish justice. Ultimately, He will bring in "a new heaven and a new earth… where there will be no more death or sorrow or crying or pain" (Revelation 21:1–4, NLT). In this eternal kingdom, "The Lord God

Almighty and the Lamb are its temple" (Revelation 21:22, AMP).

Christ's coming is not quiet or symbolic—it is the final fulfillment of God's promise to redeem and reign. He is the Alpha and Omega, and every knee will bow before Him (Philippians 2:10–11).

MORMONISM

Mormon doctrine presents a very different view of the end times and eternal destiny. According to Doctrine and Covenants 76 and Gospel Principles (Chapter 46), Mormons believe in multiple "degrees of glory", the celestial, terrestrial, and telestial kingdoms, rather than the single eternal heaven of Scripture.

They teach that after death, spirits go to either paradise or spirit prison. Those in paradise can serve as missionaries to the spirits in prison, offering them a "second chance" to accept Mormon teachings and temple ordinances before the final judgment (Doctrine and Covenants 138:30–35). This differs from the Bible's clear statement that "each person is destined to die once and after that comes judgment" (Hebrews 9:27, NLT).

Mormonism also teaches that during the Millennium, faithful Latter-day Saints will continue temple work for the dead and that exalted couples may eventually become gods themselves, creating new worlds and spirit children (Doctrine and Covenants 132:20). This teaching conflicts with Isaiah 43:10 (NLT): "Before me there was no God formed, nor will there be one after me."

While the Bible centers end-time hope on the return of Christ alone, Mormonism centers it on human progression, temple ordinances, and eternal family expansion. The contrast is clear: the Bible exalts the Lamb who reigns forever; Mormonism exalts man's potential to become like God.

POLYGAMY

From the beginning, God's design for marriage was clear and singular. Scripture teaches that marriage is a covenant between one man and one woman, joined together as "one flesh" (Genesis 2:24, NLT). God said, "This explains why a man leaves his father and mother and is joined to his wife, and the two are united into one" (Genesis 2:24, NLT). The plural "wives" was never part of His original plan.

Although instances of polygamy appear in the Old Testament, these are records of human behavior, not divine commands. God's allowance is not God's approval. Abraham took Hagar at Sarah's urging (Genesis 16:1–4), but this led to deep conflict and heartache, not blessing. Isaac, by contrast, had only one wife, Rebekah (Genesis 24:67), aligning with God's standard of faithfulness.

Kings who multiplied wives were specifically warned against doing so: "The king must not take many wives for himself, because they will turn his heart away from the Lord" (Deuteronomy 17:17, NLT). Solomon disobeyed this command and suffered the consequence of spiritual compromise: "In Solomon's old age, they turned his heart to worship other gods instead of being completely faithful to the Lord his God" (1 Kings 11:4, NLT).

By the time of the New Testament, God reaffirms monogamy as His divine design. Church leaders were to model this: "A church leader must be faithful to his wife,

and he must manage his children and household well" (1
Timothy 3:12, NLT). The Apostle Paul quotes Genesis
again, underscoring that this one-flesh union is a picture of
Christ and the Church: "As the Scriptures say, 'A man
leaves his father and mother and is joined to his wife, and
the two are united into one.' This is a great mystery, but it
is an illustration of the way Christ and the church are one"
(Ephesians 5:31–32, NLT).

God allowed polygamy in ancient times as an act
of mercy to protect women who could not provide for
themselves, but He never commanded it. The New
Covenant restores marriage to God's original plan, a
faithful, exclusive, and spiritual union between one man
and one woman.

Finally, God's blessing to Adam and Eve to "be
fruitful and multiply" (Genesis 1:28, NLT) was a blessing,
not a command to pursue sexual relationships with
multiple partners. Marriage is meant to reflect God's
covenant faithfulness, not human ambition.

In summary, Scripture makes it plain:

- God's design for marriage is monogamy
  (Genesis 2:24).
- Polygamy was tolerated but not approved
  (Deuteronomy 17:17).
- Christ restores marriage to its original design
  (Ephesians 5:31–32).
- Church leaders and believers alike are called to
  faithfulness (1 Timothy 3:12).

MORMONISM

In contrast, early *Mormonism* formally taught that
plural marriage (polygamy) was a commandment from

God, a requirement for exaltation in the afterlife. This teaching is recorded in Doctrine and Covenants 132, a revelation claimed by Joseph Smith in 1843.

The section begins by asserting that God justified ancient patriarchs in taking "many wives and concubines" (D&C 132:1–2). It then establishes plural marriage as part of the "new and everlasting covenant," warning that those who reject it "shall be damned" (D&C 132:4).

The doctrine further teaches that plural marriage is essential for godhood: "Then shall they be gods, because they have no end... then shall they be above all" (D&C 132:20). The purpose of taking multiple wives is said to be "to multiply and replenish the earth" and for "their exaltation in the eternal worlds" (D&C 132:63).

Perhaps most troubling is the personal command to Joseph Smith's wife, Emma, in verses 52–54: she is told to accept all the wives "given unto [Joseph]," or else "she shall be destroyed." This coercive revelation binds Emma to submit to a system that promised exaltation but threatened destruction for dissent.

Joseph Smith justified this doctrine by citing Old Testament figures such as Abraham, Isaac, Jacob, Moses, David, and Solomon. However, this claim collapses under biblical examination:

- Abraham was never commanded by God to take Hagar (Genesis 16:1–4).
- Isaac had only one wife, Rebekah.
- Moses had one wife at a time, first Zipporah, then a Cushite woman after her death (Numbers 12:1).

- David and Solomon had many wives, but Scripture condemns their example (1 Kings 11:3–4).

Thus, Joseph Smith's justification contradicts the biblical record. What God tolerated in history, He never prescribed as holy doctrine. Modern Mormon leaders now disavow the practice, but believe it will happen in the heavenlies. The doctrine remains canonized in Doctrine and Covenants 132. Early LDS leaders, including Brigham Young, publicly taught that exaltation required plural marriage, calling monogamy "a false and corrupt system."

Whereas the Bible presents marriage as a sacred, faithful covenant that reflects the relationship between Christ and His Church, Mormonism once tied marriage to the pursuit of deification, a path to "becoming gods" through eternal increase.

LITERAL OR FIGURATIVE

CHRISTIANITY

In his teaching The Maze of Mormonism, Christian theologian Walter Martin exposed one of the greatest misunderstandings in Mormon theology, the tendency to interpret Scripture in a hyper-literal way. He pointed out that Mormons often describe God as having a physical body: eyes, hands, arms, and even fingers.

Martin humorously addressed this by saying, "If we interpret every description of God literally, then according to Psalm 91:4, He must have feathers and wings!" Scripture says, "He will cover you with his feathers. He will shelter you with his wings. His faithful promises are your armor and protection" (Psalm 91:4, NLT). Of course, no Christian believes God is a bird. This poetic language paints a picture of His tender protection, not His anatomy.

Throughout the Bible, God uses human and earthly images to describe His invisible nature. When Jesus said, "I am the bread of life" (John 6:48, NLT), He was not suggesting that He was literally a loaf of bread. Instead, He revealed that He is the spiritual nourishment every soul needs. The Lord's words are full of imagery that helps the human mind grasp eternal truths.

The Bible teaches clearly that God is not a physical being.

"God is not a man, so he does not lie. He is not human, so he does not change his mind" (Numbers 23:19, NLT).

"God is **Spirit**, so those who worship him must worship in spirit and in truth" (John 4:24, NLT).

From Genesis to Revelation, Scripture reveals that God is eternal, invisible, and unchanging. Yet in His great love, He became visible in the person of Jesus Christ.

"The Word became human and made his home among us. He was full of unfailing love and faithfulness" (John 1:14, NLT).

The incarnation, God becoming man, is unique in all of Scripture. Jesus, the eternal Son, took on flesh not because God is material, but because humanity could never reach God on its own. The invisible became visible so that the lost could be redeemed through His blood.

Isaiah 55:11 (NLT) reminds us that God's Word never fails:

"It is the same with my word. I send it out, and it always produces fruit. It will accomplish all I want it to."

In other words, Scripture accomplishes its divine purpose when interpreted in its intended sense—using proper context, literary form, and the full revelation of Christ. Christians are called to interpret figurative language symbolically, not literally, when the context clearly demands it.

The Bible's metaphors reveal who God is, not what He looks like. He is Spirit, eternal, and perfect in being, yet He lovingly made Himself known through the incarnation of Jesus Christ.

MORMONISM

In contrast, *Mormon* theology, found in its own canon of scriptures such as the Doctrine and Covenants and the Book of Mormon, teaches that God the Father is an exalted man with a physical body. The Doctrine and Covenants describes God as having a tangible form and existing within space and time.

This literalism extends beyond the person of God to the interpretation of Scripture. For example, whereas Christianity understands poetic and symbolic passages (like Psalm 91:4) as metaphors revealing God's attributes, Mormonism often treats these expressions as literal descriptions of divine characteristics. This approach reflects a major theological divide.

According to Mormon teaching, the Heavenly Father and the Son are two distinct embodied beings united in purpose but separate in substance. In contrast, biblical theology teaches that the Father, Son, and Holy Spirit are one God in three persons, eternally coequal and coeternal.

Mormonism also emphasizes human exaltation, the belief that faithful members may become gods themselves in the afterlife, possessing glory and creative power like the Father. This belief is reinforced in *Doctrine and Covenants 132:20:*

"Then shall they be gods, because they have no end; therefore shall they be from everlasting to everlasting."

In LDS theology, this literal, physical conception of God ties directly to its broader system of exaltation and celestial progression. By contrast, Christianity teaches that salvation makes believers children of God by adoption, not gods by nature (Romans 8:15–17, NLT). We share in His glory by grace, not by self-exaltation.

Furthermore, *Mormonism's* acceptance of ongoing revelation through modern prophets allows its doctrine to reinterpret Scripture and sometimes override the Bible's clear teaching. In this way, anthropomorphic language, originally intended to help humans understand divine attributes, becomes the foundation for an entire theology that depicts God as once mortal and still embodied.

Walter Martin's critique reminds believers of the importance of sound interpretation. To take the Bible literally where it is figurative is to miss the beauty and truth of its message. The Bible is rich in symbolism, divine revelation communicated through human language, but always points to one eternal truth:

God is Spirit. He is eternal, invisible, and unchanging, revealed perfectly in Jesus Christ, the visible image of the invisible God (Colossians 1:15, NLT).

Christian theology upholds both God's transcendence and His immanence. He is near to us, yet above us. He is beyond the physical world, yet entered it to redeem us.

The challenge of Mormonism's literalism is not just in its misunderstanding of Scripture's language, it is in its misunderstanding of who God is. Christians must therefore hold fast to biblical revelation:

"God is not a man" (Numbers 23:19, NLT).
"God is Spirit" (John 4:24, NLT).
"The Word became human and made his home among us" (John 1:14, NLT).

This is the mystery and glory of the gospel, the eternal Spirit became flesh to bring us life.

PLANS

CHRISTIANITY

The Bible teaches that human life begins in God's creative act, not in a premortal world. Paul writes, "When Adam sinned, sin entered the world… so death spread to everyone, for everyone sinned" (Romans 5:12, NLT). God then sent his son to die for those sins, to be a substitute for us, lifting the curse given to Adam. Salvation is therefore God's gift in Christ, not the memory of a righteous choice made before birth.

Paul's phrase "terrestrial bodies and bodies celestial" is often misunderstood. When Paul speaks of "bodies in the heavens and bodies on the earth" (1 Corinthians 15:40, NLT), he describes the difference between earthly and resurrected bodies, not levels of heaven. Terrestrial in the Greek language is "epigeios" meaning **existing upon the earth**. Celestial in the Greek language is "epouranios" meaning **existing in heaven** (The New Testament was written in Greek, where this verse is found).

Scripture never outlines three degrees of glory. Instead, it promises a single renewed creation: "Then I saw a new heaven and a new earth" (Revelation 21:1, NLT). In that new world, God gives "water of life without cost" (Revelation 21:6, NLT), and His people "will see His face" (Revelation 22:4, NLT). This is the Christian hope, one heaven, one people, one eternal inheritance.

Believers trust God's leading, not a mapped-out system. "Trust in the Lord with all your heart… and he will show you which path to take" (Proverbs 3:5–6, NLT). Salvation rests entirely on His grace.

MORMONISM

Mormon Latter-day Saint doctrine teaches a premortal life where humans existed as spirit children who chose Jesus instead of Satan before earthly birth. It also presents three kingdoms of glory, celestial, terrestrial, and *telestial*, a uniquely LDS-created term, first introduced in *Doctrine and Covenants 76* to describe the lowest of the three kingdoms of glory. (It is important to note that this term *telestial* does not appear in any Bible translation, early Christian writings, Greek or Hebrew manuscripts, historical theological sources, or even <u>English dictionaries</u> before Mormon usage).

Advancement within these kingdoms, especially the highest degree of the celestial kingdom, depends on LDS ordinances such as temple endowments, baptisms for the dead, and eternal marriage.

Where LDS theology offers a graded plan of salvation, the Bible offers God's single, gracious promise to all who belong to Christ. It's not a plan, HE IS THE PLAN.

GRACE

God's love for us is vast, beyond imagination, beyond measurement. Scripture reveals a God whose thoughts toward His children are so innumerable they surpass the sands of the sea.

"Your eyes saw my unformed body; all the days ordained for me were written in your book before one of them came to be" (Psalm 139:16, ESV).

"How precious are your thoughts about me, O God. They cannot be numbered!" (Psalm 139:17, NLT).

"If I were to count them, they would outnumber the grains of sand; and when I awake, I am still with You" (Psalm 139:18, BSB).

These verses remind us that God's awareness of us is both personal and infinite. He sees every detail, ordains every day, and sustains every breath. His love is more vast than the ocean—eternal, constant, and undeserved. His grace truly is sufficient (2 Corinthians 12:9, NLT).

When we meditate on His greatness, we echo Job's awe:

"If he commands it, the sun won't rise and the stars won't shine" (Job 9:7, NLT).

"He alone stretches out the heavens and treads on the waves of the sea" (Job 9:8, NIV).

"He performs wonders that cannot be fathomed, miracles that cannot be counted" (Job 9:10, NIV).

This God, so powerful, yet so near, is not a distant deity but a personal Father who calls us to rest in His love and trust in His timing. His thoughts and ways are far above ours (Isaiah 55:8, NLT), and yet His care reaches into our daily lives. His timing is never late, even when we feel we are waiting long. As with Abraham and Sarah, His promises are sure, even when human logic says otherwise.

God's grace is not earned by human effort or religious performance. Scripture teaches,

"A person is made right with God by faith in Jesus Christ, not by obeying the law" (Galatians 2:16, NLT).

We are not justified by "works of the law" but by faith alone in Christ. The Old Covenant law revealed human sin and the need for a Savior, while the New Covenant fulfills that law through love. Jesus summarized the entire law in two commands:

"You must love the Lord your God with all your heart, all your soul, and all your mind. This is the first and greatest commandment. A second is equally important: Love your neighbor as yourself" (Matthew 22:37–39, NLT).

True faith naturally produces good works, not as a means of salvation, but as its fruit (James 2:26). Good works flow from a heart transformed by grace. They are evidence, not currency. The believer's life is one of response, not performance.

Christ's death on the cross completed every work necessary for salvation. The message of the cross may seem foolish to some, but to us who are being saved, it is the power of God (1 Corinthians 1:18, NLT).

Through Jesus, grace is immediate and available now—not after judgment, not after self-cleansing. He invites sinners to come, believe, and receive forgiveness today. He bore our sin willingly so that we might be free.

"God so loved the world that he gave his one and only Son, so that everyone who believes in him will not perish but have eternal life" (John 3:16, NLT).

When we rest in that love, we live out of acceptance rather than striving. Grace is unearned favor, a gift freely given. Mercy is withheld judgment, a punishment not given though deserved. Both meet at the cross.

To live in grace means to accept that the work of salvation is finished. To deny grace is to deny the cross. Jesus' blood, His sacrifice, and His resurrection are the foundation of eternal life. The believer's "works" are no longer religious duties but grateful acts of love empowered by the Holy Spirit.

MORMONISM

In *Mormon scripture, The Book of Moses in the Pearl of Great Price* portrays a different picture of God's creation and grace. In Moses 1:33–37, God says,

"And worlds without number have I created… there are many worlds that have passed away by the word of my power… and innumerable are they unto man; but all things are numbered unto me, for they are mine."

This teaching introduces a cosmology of many earths and heavens, expanding beyond the singular creation described in Genesis.

The Bible speaks of one heaven and one earth, created by one God for His redemptive purpose, not "worlds without number."

Mormonism also differs sharply on the doctrine of grace and works. While Scripture teaches justification by faith alone (Galatians 2:16), LDS theology teaches that faith must be accompanied by personal righteousness and enduring obedience to the commandments in order to achieve exaltation. In practice, this creates a system of continual striving, what the LDS call "enduring to the end."

In Mormon culture, grace is often viewed as a tool to help one become worthy, rather than the unearned favor that saves. The focus remains on moral progress rather than complete redemption through the cross. Because the LDS Church does not emphasize the cross as a saving symbol, but the living Christ instead, many Latter-day Saints view the crucifixion as a tragic death rather than the completed act of atonement.

This perspective diminishes the power of the finished work of Jesus. As the Apostle Paul warned,

"They stumbled over the great rock in their path. God warned them… 'I am placing a stone in Jerusalem that makes people stumble… but anyone who trusts in him will never be disgraced'" (Romans 9:32–33, NLT).

By relying on human merit, Mormonism reintroduces the "law of works" that Christ came to fulfill.

It replaces rest with endless labor, religious effort in place of spiritual surrender.

Mormon doctrine of exaltation, described in Doctrine and Covenants 132, teaches that those who obey the ordinances perfectly can become gods themselves. Yet Scripture proclaims, "There is no other God; there never has been and there never will be" (Isaiah 43:10, NLT).

The gospel of Jesus Christ calls us not to self-exaltation, but to humble acceptance of His grace. Salvation is not delayed until death or judgment; it is received the moment faith meets repentance. Grace transforms now.

God's love is deeper than the ocean and more numerous than the grains of sand. His grace is sufficient, His plan eternal, His mercy undeserved. When we receive His love, we rest, not strive.

Our good works are not wages earned, but worship offered. The only "work" left for the believer is the work of faith, to believe in the One God sent (John 6:29, NLT). We love Him because He first loved us (1 John 4:19). That is grace.

DEMONS

CHRISTIANITY

Scripture presents the spiritual world as real, active, and deeply connected to human life. Demons are not symbols but fallen angels who oppose God and seek to harm His creation. When the Lord asked Satan where he had been, Satan answered, "From roaming the earth and going back and forth on it" (Job 2:2, NLT). His activity is ongoing, and the New Testament confirms his intent to destroy. Peter describes him as "a roaring lion, looking for someone to devour" (1 Peter 5:8, NLT).

Believers take these realities seriously because God does not change. If His Word is true, then the spiritual battles described in Scripture remain present today. Christ grants authority over demons to those who belong to Him, not through personal strength but through His name alone. John teaches, "But to all who believed him and accepted him, he gave the right to become children of God" (John 1:12, NLT). Becoming God's child is a gift of grace, not a natural birthright, for Adam's sin has affected every person born into the world (Romans 5:12, NLT).

Demons torment through fear, deception, and accusation, yet their power is broken by Christ. Jesus sends His people "as sheep among wolves" (Matthew 10:16, NLT), not to stand in their own ability but to remain dependent on Him. Deliverance belongs to the Lord. Only Christ casts out darkness because only Christ reigns over it.

MORMONISM

Mormon Latter-day Saint teachings acknowledge the existence of Satan and affirm that one-third of heaven followed him in rebellion. Yet LDS doctrine minimizes the ongoing activity of demons. Official materials often present Satan as limited primarily to persuasion rather than spiritual oppression, possession, or direct torment. The Book of Mormon speaks of the devil leading hearts astray (*1 Nephi 14:7*) but does not portray demonic activity as Scripture describes it, active, destructive, and requiring divine deliverance.

In *Mormon LDS* theology, humanity begins as premortal spirit children of God who enter mortality already aligned with Him, weakening the biblical teaching that all people are born under Adam's fall and spiritually vulnerable apart from Christ (Romans 5:12, NLT). Because LDS doctrine views humans as inherently divine in origin, it does not emphasize the biblical need for Christ's authority over demonic forces. The result is a diminished understanding of spiritual warfare. Where the Bible presents a world in which demons torment, deceive, and must be cast out by the power of Jesus, LDS teaching often reduces Satan to a tempter without real dominion.

The Christian confession is clear: without belonging to Christ, a person has no spiritual authority over the enemy. But the moment one becomes a child of God through faith, the darkness must submit to the name of Jesus.

TEMPLE

CHRISTIANITY

The Bible teaches that the true temple of God is no longer a physical building but the hearts of believers indwelt by the Holy Spirit. In the Old Testament, the temple was where God's presence dwelt and sacrifices were made for sin. These rituals foreshadowed Jesus Christ, whose death and resurrection fulfilled the entire temple system (Hebrews 9:11–12, NLT).

Jesus revealed that worship would no longer depend on a location:

> "But the time is coming, indeed it's here now, when true worshipers will worship the Father in spirit and in truth" (John 4:23, NLT).

After His resurrection, the Church became His body, the living temple of God.

> "Don't you realize that all of you together are the temple of God and that the Spirit of God lives in you?" (1 Corinthians 3:16, NLT).
> "He is the God who made the world and everything in it… he doesn't live in man-made temples" (Acts 17:24, NLT).

When Jesus died, the veil in the temple was torn (Matthew 27:51), symbolizing full access to God through Christ. His sacrifice made every believer a living temple. Paul urged believers to live holy lives, offering themselves as "living and holy sacrifices" (Romans 12:1, NLT).

The Old Testament tabernacle pointed to Christ in every detail:

- The door taught there is only one way to God, fulfilled in Jesus, "I am the door" (John 10:9).
- The altar symbolized atonement, fulfilled in Jesus, "I give my life a ransom for many" (Mark 10:45).
- The veil showed separation, fulfilled when Jesus tore it and gave direct access to God (Hebrews 10:20).

Now, through Christ, believers have direct communion with the Father. "For there is one God and one mediator who can reconcile God and humanity, the man Christ Jesus" (1 Timothy 2:5, NLT).

God does not dwell in temples built by hands; He dwells within His people. "Heaven is my throne, and the earth is my footstool. Could you build me a temple as good as that?" (Isaiah 66:1, NLT).

MORMONISM

In contrast, *Mormons* continue to build physical temples, calling them "the house of the Lord." These temples are central to LDS worship, where members perform ordinances such as baptisms for the dead, eternal marriage sealings, and endowment ceremonies. Only those who pass worthiness interviews receive a "temple recommend" to enter, something never required in Scripture.

Mormon leaders interpret Jesus' words in Matthew 16:19 ("Whatever you bind on earth shall be bound in heaven") as justification for temple ordinances. Yet Jesus' statement referred to the authority to declare the gospel, not to perform rituals for the dead. Christ Himself taught, "When the dead rise, they will neither marry nor be given in marriage" (Matthew 22:30, NLT).

The temple rituals in Mormonism find no basis in the New Testament. Instead, they reflect post-biblical developments and similarities to Freemasonic ceremonies introduced by Joseph Smith in 1842. These man-made forms attempt to continue what Christ already completed.

The LDS Church claims temple work connects families eternally and advances salvation. But the Bible teaches that salvation is by faith alone, not by ordinance or structure. "God saved you by his grace when you believed. And you can't take credit for this; it is a gift from God" (Ephesians 2:8, NLT).

By emphasizing temples of stone, Mormonism reverses the finished work of the cross, where God tore the veil and made His dwelling within believers. Scripture says plainly, "We are the temple of the living God" (2 Corinthians 6:16, NLT).

Christ fulfilled all that the temple represented. He is the High Priest who entered the heavenly temple once for all (Hebrews 9:12). No temple made with human hands can contain His glory.

HEAVENLY FATHER OR FATHER GOD

CHRISTIANITY

God is not merely an earthly father figure, He is the Creator of all things. Unlike human fathers who reproduce through natural means, God spoke life into existence. Scripture teaches, "For we are God's masterpiece. He has created us anew in Christ Jesus, so we can do the good things he planned for us long ago" (Ephesians 2:10, NLT).

When we plant a seed, we may water it, but we do not create life itself. As Paul wrote, "I planted the seed, Apollos watered it, but God has been making it grow" (1 Corinthians 3:6, NLT). Creation belongs to God alone.

Jesus' miraculous conception, born of a virgin, reveals that God entered humanity not through natural procreation, but through divine power (Luke 1:35). This demonstrated His role as both Creator and Redeemer, drawing people to the humble place of His birth, where the promised Messiah entered the world in perfect sovereignty.

Just as parents prepare a safe space for a baby, God prepared a world where His children could freely choose Him. Even when we find ourselves in painful or confusing circumstances, He uses those places for our awakening. He knows every situation we would face, including being born into false systems or broken homes, and He uses them to call us out and into truth. "For God so loved the world, that he gave his only Son, that whoever believes in him should not perish but have eternal life" (John 3:16, NLT).

God's love is different from human love. Earthly fathers, though well-intentioned, are imperfect. Some may be harsh, distant, or controlling, but God is not like that. Scripture says, "You received God's Spirit when he adopted you as his own children. Now we call him, 'Abba, Father'" (Romans 8:15, NLT). Our relationship with Him is not through fear or performance but through adoption by grace.

He instructs His children through His Word, not through human manipulation. "Older men are to be temperate, dignified, self-controlled, sound in faith… Older women likewise… to teach what is good… that they may train the younger women… and encourage the younger men" (Titus 2:1–8, NLT). God's order for family and growth begins with sound doctrine, not tradition or control.

Parents are entrusted to reflect the love of the true Father. "Fathers, do not provoke your children, lest they become discouraged" (Colossians 3:21, NLT). When children are pointed toward the Bible, not human approval, they grow confident in God's identity rather than seeking it from man.

This is the heart of Christian life, relationship with the Creator who loves us perfectly. "For God has not given us a spirit of fear, but of power, love, and self-discipline" (2 Timothy 1:7, NLT). Through faith in Christ, believers learn to rest in His fatherly care, knowing that His authority is loving, not oppressive. God is not a reflection of human fathers—He is our perfect Creator and Redeemer. He adopts us into His family through faith in

Christ, giving us security, identity, and purpose. His love is not earned through works but received through grace.

MORMONISM

Mormon scripture and song teaches that all humans are literal spirit children of Heavenly Father and Heavenly Mother, born in a pre-earth existence before coming to earth. The Primary song *"I Am a Child of God"* reflects this belief:

"I am a child of God,
And he has sent me here,
Has given me an earthly home
With parents kind and dear.
Teach me all that I must do
To live with him someday."

The phrase *"teach me all that I must do"* emphasizes works as a condition for returning to God, a theme repeated throughout Mormon doctrine. Moroni 10:32 in the Book of Mormon says: "If ye shall deny yourselves of all ungodliness… then is his grace sufficient for you." Grace, according to this view, is conditional, available only after full obedience.

The *Mormon song "I Lived in Heaven"* also teaches preexistence:

"I lived in heaven a long time ago, it is true;
Lived there and loved there with people I know. So did
you."

This directly contradicts the Bible, which teaches that human life begins on earth when God forms and breathes life into us (Genesis 2:7). This is also clearly laid out in 1 Corinthians 15:46 NIV, "The spiritual did not come first, but the natural, and after that the spiritual."

The concept of a "Heavenly Mother" and a pre-earth life has no biblical foundation and redefines the Creator-creature relationship by making humanity eternal and self-existent rather than created.

Mormon doctrine also limits God's fatherhood to those who obey LDS commandments and temple covenants. According to The Family: A Proclamation to the World (1995), exaltation, becoming like God and living eternally with one's family, is possible only through temple ordinances and adherence to LDS teachings.

In contrast, Scripture teaches that adoption into God's family is not earned by worthiness or ritual but is granted freely through Christ. "To all who believed him and accepted him, he gave the right to become children of God" (John 1:12, NLT). Salvation is not based on perfection or endurance, but on grace alone through faith (Ephesians 2:8–9).

Mormonism teaches that people are literal spirit offspring of Heavenly Parents and must prove worthiness through obedience and ordinances to regain God's presence. The Bible teaches that God alone is the Creator, that we are His workmanship, and that we become His children by adoption through Jesus Christ, not by birthright or works. Grace is God's gift, not a reward for human effort.

IDOLS

CHRISTIANITY

The God of the Bible is supernatural, eternal, and wholly sufficient. He is uncreated and sovereign over all creation. Humans are His creatures, distinct from Him, dependent on His power for life and growth. As Ephesians 2:10 (NLT) states, "For we are God's masterpiece. He has created us anew in Christ Jesus, so we can do the good things he planned for us long ago." Human action is valuable, but God alone gives increase:

> "I planted the seed, Apollos watered it, but God has been making it grow. So neither the one who plants nor the one who waters is anything, but only God, who makes things grow" (1 Corinthians 3:6–7, NLT).

Jesus Christ, fully God and fully man, entered the world to accomplish salvation, independent of human effort (John 3:16; Matthew 20:28, NLT). Salvation is a gift of grace, received by faith, not earned by works. Believers are adopted as God's children (Romans 8:15, NLT), secure in His love and called to obedience out of gratitude, not necessity.

God judges those who turn to idle worship, yet He is merciful-sending both Jonah and Nahum to warn Nineveh over a century apart. But because the people refused to repent, Nineveh was ultimately destroyed.

The twelve disciples exemplify faithful obedience without becoming objects of worship. They follow Christ and are transformed by Him, yet all glory points to God, not to the men themselves. Their value lies in their relationship with Jesus, not in their physical stature, military strength, or heroic exploits.

Believers are empowered through the Spirit (Philippians 4:13, NLT), restored and strengthened by God's Word (Hebrews 9:12–14, NLT), and called to live as representatives of His love and truth (Colossians 2:9–10, NLT). The Bible provides both vertical relationship with God and horizontal guidance through Christ's example, yet the disciples themselves are never worshiped; they are followers of the Lord, not idols.

MORMONISM

In contrast, *the Book of Mormon* emphasizes human heroism and performance as a reflection of divine favor. Figures such as Nephi, Helaman, Moroni, Ammon, and others are depicted as physically imposing, militarily skilled, and morally heroic (*Book of Mormon, Helaman 3–5; Alma 17–18*). These characters are often represented visually in LDS culture, statues, paintings, and songs, creating models for admiration and emulation.

Mormon instruction, including songs like *"We Are as the Armies of Helaman,"* reinforces the idea that spiritual success is tied to courage, action, and physical or moral prowess. Ammon's defense of King Lamoni's flocks by severing the arms of robbers (*Alma 17:29–39, Book of Mormon*) exemplifies the expectation of heroic action as a demonstration of righteousness. Salvation is framed as contingent upon obedience, ritual, and performance (*Moroni 10:32, Book of Mormon*).

Mormon doctrine further emphasizes preexistence, exaltation, and the potential for humans to become like

God. Individuals are seen as eternal spirit children of a Heavenly Father, with their spiritual status linked to works, ordinances, and missionary service (*The Family: A Proclamation to the World, 1995*). The emphasis on human heroism contrasts with biblical Christianity, where God's work is complete and human action is a response, not a requirement.

While biblical disciples are models of faithful obedience pointing to Christ, Book of Mormon figures are often idolized for their strength, courage, and deeds. The focus shifts from God to human exemplars, creating a culture where man's actions and achievements are central to spiritual identity.

Understanding this contrast is vital for instruction. Biblical Christianity encourages believers to focus on God as the source of strength, guidance, and righteousness (1 Corinthians 3:7, NLT). True worship honors God alone, not human exemplars, and faith rests on Christ's finished work. In teaching and ministry, pointing hearts to God, rather than to human models, nurtures dependence on divine grace, not human effort.

THE WEDDING

Our walk with God is often described in Scripture as a covenant like marriage, where Christ is the Bridegroom and the Church is His bride (Ephesians 5:25–27, NLT). Just as in marriage, following Christ must come from free will and personal choice. A believer cannot rely on someone else's faith or strength to walk them to the altar of commitment. Salvation is a personal covenant between each soul and Christ.

Paul wrote, "When I was a child, I spoke and thought and reasoned as a child. But when I grew up, I put away childish things" (1 Corinthians 13:11, NLT). Spiritually maturing means walking with God by our own faith, choosing Him daily, not through another's influence.

Peter also urged believers, "You must live as God's obedient children. Don't slip back into your old ways of living to satisfy your own desires. You didn't know any better then" (1 Peter 1:14, NLT). This faith is refined by trials, producing maturity and steadfast love for Christ. "So be truly glad. There is wonderful joy ahead, even though you must endure many trials for a little while" (1 Peter 1:6, NLT). Through these trials, our faith is proven genuine, resulting in "the salvation of your souls" (1 Peter 1:9, NLT).

In Scripture, the wedding symbolizes readiness and devotion. Jesus told the parable of the wise and foolish virgins, some were prepared with oil in their lamps, others were not (Matthew 25:1–13, NLT). The prepared ones entered the wedding feast, representing believers who walk faithfully with Christ until His return.

Marriage on earth mirrors this divine relationship. A Christian wedding is a public declaration of an inward covenant, made before God, not dependent on ritual but on the heart's obedience and love. Husbands and wives are called to reflect Christ and His Church, teaching their children in the way they should go (Ephesians 5:25–33; Proverbs 22:6, NLT).

MORMONISM

Mormon doctrine teaches that marriage must be performed by priesthood authority in a temple to be valid for eternity. Couples wear specific temple garments and participate in rituals involving symbolic clothing, veils, and kneeling at an altar before witnesses to be "sealed" for time and eternity (Doctrine and Covenants 132:19). This practice is presented as necessary for exaltation, the highest level of salvation in Mormon belief.

The Book of Mormon and Doctrine and Covenants emphasize temple ordinances and eternal marriage as conditions for achieving godhood and dwelling with family in the celestial kingdom (Doctrine and Covenants 131:1–4). Thus, marriage becomes a requirement necessary for salvation rather than a covenant of grace.

In contrast, the Bible teaches that marriage, while sacred, is not a condition for eternal life. Salvation is by grace through faith in Christ alone (Ephesians 2:8–9, NLT). Paul even stated, "I wish everyone were single, just as I am… An unmarried man can spend his time doing the Lord's work and thinking how to please Him" (1 Corinthians 7:7, 32, NLT).

The Christian view points to a spiritual union with Christ that surpasses earthly ceremony, where the true "wedding" is between the Savior and His redeemed people.

DEBT- A MONEY METAPHOR

Paul teaches that every believer once stood guilty before God, condemned by sin, but was declared righteous through faith in Jesus Christ. "But now God has shown us a way to be made right with him without keeping the requirements of the law… We are made right with God by placing our faith in Jesus Christ" (Romans 3:21–22, NLT). Christ paid the price in full; nothing can be added or earned.

The metaphor of payment describes God's justice and mercy. Sin created a debt; the wages of sin is death (Romans 6:23, NLT). Yet Christ satisfied that debt by His sacrifice. "He has appeared once for all time to remove sin by his own death as a sacrifice" (Hebrews 9:26, NLT). Salvation is not a recurring payment plan; it is a completed transaction sealed by grace.

Jesus explained that wealth often blinds the heart: "It is easier for a camel to go through the eye of a needle than for a rich person to enter the Kingdom of God" (Matthew 19:24, NLT). The true riches of heaven are not earned but received by faith. God's economy runs on surrender, not status.

Consumerism and pride feed a false sense of security. Scripture reminds us that "the borrower is servant to the lender" (Proverbs 22:7, NLT). The Lord calls His people to freedom; financial, spiritual, and moral, by trusting Him as provider. Jesus said, "I have a kind of food you know nothing about" (John 4:32, NLT), showing that His nourishment came from doing the Father's will.

Isaiah wrote, "My ways are far beyond anything you could imagine" (Isaiah 55:9, NLT). God uses familiar words like money, payment, and debt to explain divine truths, but His goal is revelation, not riddle. When we walk in faith, the Word comes alive; the believer reads Scripture through the eyes of Christ, understanding that redemption is finished and freely given.

MORMONISM

Latter-day Saint (LDS) doctrine teaches that Christ's atonement made resurrection possible, but individuals must perform ordinances and obey laws to fully receive exaltation. Salvation in the LDS sense includes multiple degrees of glory, with exaltation (becoming gods) and eternal life granted only to those who enter temple covenants and remain obedient (Doctrine and Covenants 76:50–70; 132:19–20).

In *Mormon* belief, Christ's payment was not complete on behalf of all; members must continue making spiritual "payments" through temple work, tithing, and personal worthiness to maintain their standing. The Book of Mormon teaches that "it is by grace that we are saved, after all we can do" (2 Nephi 25:23). Thus, grace functions as an aid following personal effort, not as the sole basis for justification.

In contrast, the Bible proclaims that justification is a finished act of God through faith alone. "God saved you by his grace when you believed. And you can't take credit for this; it is a gift from God" (Ephesians 2:8, NLT). Salvation is not a shared project between God and man; it is a gift purchased by Christ and freely received by all who believe.

TESTIMONY

CHRISTIANITY

In Biblical scripture, a true testimony is always centered on God's glory, not human recognition. Jesus healed the man at the pool of Bethesda, later warning him, "Now you are well; so stop sinning, or something even worse may happen to you" (John 5:14, NLT). The miracle was not for fame or public display, it was for God's purpose alone.

Jesus taught Nicodemus, "You can't explain how people are born of the Spirit. The wind blows wherever it wants. Just as you can hear the wind but can't tell where it comes from or where it is going, so you can't explain how people are born of the Spirit" (John 3:8, NLT).

A true, Spirit-born testimony flows from a heart transformed by grace, not from memorized words or pressure to perform. The believer's story of salvation exalts Christ alone.

"Those who boast should boast only about the Lord." 2 Corinthians 10:17 (NLT)

MORMONISM

In the *Mormon* Church, "Fast Sunday" occurs monthly, where members skip two or three meals and donate "fast offerings." Afterward, during the Testimony

Meeting, members are invited to share personal affirmations of faith.

Typical testimonies follow a pattern taught from childhood:

1. "I know this church is true."
2. "I know Joseph Smith was a true prophet."
3. "I know the current prophet is called of God."
4. "I know families can be together forever."
5. "I know my Savior loves me."

These statements, though sincere, are uniform and rehearsed, focusing on loyalty to the LDS Church rather than spiritual rebirth through Christ. Mormon members are taught that the Holy Spirit confirms these beliefs as truth, yet they are rooted in allegiance to human prophets rather than Scripture.

In contrast, Jesus said that those born of the Spirit follow the voice of God, not man (John 3:8). The biblical testimony gives glory only to Christ; the Mormon testimony often glorifies the organization and its leaders.

THE FALL

The Bible teaches that Adam's disobedience brought sin and death into the world, and that through Christ, the "second Adam", we receive life.

"For since by man came death, by man came also the resurrection of the dead. For as in Adam all die, so also in Christ shall all be made alive." 1 Corinthians 15:21–22 (NLT)

The fall was not a noble or necessary act. Scripture clearly states that "Eve was deceived by the cunning of the serpent" (2 Corinthians 11:3, NLT). This was a real sin and a real temptation. The enemy had power to bruise humanity's heel, but Christ alone gives believers authority over the devil (Luke 10:19).

God's Word shows that Adam and Eve could have multiplied without sin. Before the fall, God said, "Be fruitful and multiply. Fill the earth and govern it" (Genesis 1:28, NLT). The consequence after sin was increased pain in childbirth—not the creation of it (Genesis 3:16). God does not lie or contradict Himself (Numbers 23:19).

Through Adam's sin, death entered humanity:

"When Adam sinned, sin entered the world. Adam's sin brought death, so death spread to everyone." Romans 5:12 (NLT)

But through Christ, the curse was reversed. His atonement restores life to all who believe. As Romans 3:23

reminds us, "For everyone has sinned; we all fall short of God's glorious standard." Yet, through faith in Christ, we are made alive. We no longer live in condemnation, but in redemption through His blood (Romans 8:1–2).

MORMONISM

Mormon doctrine interprets Adam's fall as a necessary and positive step in God's plan. The Book of Mormon states:

"Adam fell that men might be; and men are, that they might have joy." 2 Nephi 2:25

Mormon teaching views Eve's choice as courageous and inspired, claiming that humanity could not have been born without her partaking of the fruit. This redefines sin as a blessing in disguise rather than rebellion against God.

LDS Article of Faith 2 states, "*We believe that men will be punished for their own sins, and not for Adam's transgression.*" This denies the biblical truth that death entered through Adam and spread to all (Romans 5:12).

Traditional LDS thought has even suggested that faithful members can eventually progress to godhood, mirroring Adam's supposed exaltation. While modern leaders avoid open discussion of this, it remains rooted in early LDS teaching.

This doctrine removes the necessity of Christ's full atonement. If Adam's sin brought joy rather than death, then Christ's death is reduced to a symbolic act rather than the sole means of salvation. The Bible, however, teaches that "just as everyone dies because we all belong to Adam, everyone who belongs to Christ will be given new life" (1 Corinthians 15:22, NLT).

BIBLE TRANSLATIONS

CHRISTIANITY

The Bible declares itself to be God-breathed and unchanging truth. Scripture is not bound to one language or translation, because the same Spirit who inspired its words preserves its message across generations.

"All Scripture is inspired by God and is useful to teach us what is true and to make us realize what is wrong in our lives" (2 Timothy 3:16, NLT).

The Word of God is living and active (Hebrews 4:12, NLT), meaning it transcends culture and translation. God's truth is not fragile, it does not lose its meaning when expressed in modern language. Translators seek to make Scripture clear for people in every tongue and time, faithfully rendering the same truth that was written under divine inspiration.

John 3:16, in several translations, reveals this consistency:

- ASV: "For God so loved the world, that he gave his only begotten Son, that whosoever believes on him should not perish, but have eternal life."
- KJV: "For God so loved the world, that he gave his only begotten Son, that whosoever believeth in him should not perish, but have everlasting life."
- NIV: "For God so loved the world that he gave his one and only Son, that whoever believes in him shall not perish but have eternal life."

Though the phrasing changes slightly, the meaning never does: God's love is steadfast, salvation is through faith in His Son, and eternal life is His promise.

Different Bible translations are not corruptions but tools for deeper understanding. They allow believers to study context, explore Greek and Hebrew meanings, and grow in relationship with God.

The Bible's reliability is unmatched in history. With over 5,000 ancient Greek manuscripts and thousands of early translations and quotations, the New Testament has more manuscript evidence than any other ancient text—far exceeding even Homer's Iliad. God has clearly preserved His Word.

In *Mormon scripture, The Eighth Article of Faith of the LDS Church* states:

"We believe the Bible to be the word of God as far as it is translated correctly." (Articles of Faith 1:8)

This phrase introduces doubt about the Bible's authority and elevates other LDS scriptures—especially the Book of Mormon, as supposedly "more correct." Members are taught that the King James Version is the only acceptable translation, often coupled with Joseph Smith's "Inspired Version." As a result, many Mormons are discouraged from reading the Bible on its own, being told it might confuse them without the Book of Mormon to interpret it.

MORMONISM

The official LDS narrative claims that biblical truth has been lost or altered over time. *Joseph Smith's Book of Mormon (1 Nephi 13:26–29)* teaches that "*many plain and precious things*" were removed from the Bible. This assertion directly contradicts Scripture's claim that God's Word endures forever (Isaiah 40:8; Psalm 119:89).

Ironically, Joseph Smith borrowed and altered roughly a quarter of his text directly from the King James Bible. Yet, instead of upholding Scripture's authority, he claimed to restore it. The LDS position implies that God was unable to preserve His Word, a claim the Bible itself refutes.

Unlike the biblical approach, which welcomes translation and study, Mormonism restricts access to certain versions and redefines "inspiration" through its own prophets. Christians, however, rejoice in the freedom to explore Scripture through multiple faithful translations, trusting that God's Spirit safeguards His truth across languages and generations.

SAINTS

CHRISTIANITY

In Scripture, the word saint simply means someone who belongs to Jesus. Paul called ordinary believers in Ephesus "saints," not because they achieved a special status, but because they were set apart by God, not by themselves (Eph. 1:1, NLT). The Greek word 'hagios' means "set apart, holy, consecrated." This holiness is not earned, it's received. Every Christian is made holy because Jesus cleanses us from sin through His death and resurrection (Rom. 3:22–24, NLT).

The Bible uses the term saints to refer to all believers, never to a class of spiritually superior people or a group striving to earn perfection. When Jesus says, "Be perfect, therefore, as your heavenly Father is perfect" (Matt. 5:48, NLT), He is calling His followers to reflect God's love, not achieve sinless moral perfection through human effort. Our perfection is found in Christ alone (Heb. 10:14, NLT). We are saints because God adopts us as His children, places His Spirit within us, and sets us apart for Himself.

In Scripture, the emphasis is always on what God does, not on what people achieve. Being a saint is a gift of grace, rooted in God's love, not human performance.

MORMONISM

The Mormon Church or Church of Jesus Christ of Latter-day Saints uses the title "Latter-Day Saints" to identify its members as the restored, end-times people of

God. In *LDS* teaching, saints are those who belong to the restored church and keep its commandments, ordinances, and covenants. Their identity as saints is tied to loyalty to the LDS Church and progression toward exaltation through obedience, temple worthiness, and covenant-keeping *(Doctrine and Covenants 1:30; 82:10)*.

While the Bible teaches that believers are saints because of Christ's finished work, LDS teaching links "saint" with achieving higher righteousness, becoming worthy, and ultimately striving toward perfection and exaltation. Passages such as "be ye therefore perfect" (Matt. 5:48) are interpreted in LDS doctrine as commandments to work toward personal perfection as part of the eternal progression required for exaltation *(Book of Mormon, 3 Nephi 12:48)*.

In *LDS* belief, the phrase "Latter-Day Saints" also reflects the claim that the LDS Church is the only true and authorized church on earth (*Doctrine and Covenants 1:30*). By using the name of Jesus Christ in the title, the LDS Church teaches that Christ sustains this one institution above all others. Salvation and exaltation, in LDS teaching, come only through accepting Mormonism, receiving LDS ordinances, and remaining faithful to its commandments.

In contrast, the Bible offers a different foundation. Christians are saints because Jesus lives in them, saves them by grace, and sets them apart as His children, not because they elevate themselves through religious achievement.

SATAN

Before we talk about Satan, lets talk about Jesus. The Bible teaches that Jesus Christ is the eternal Creator, fully divine and uncreated. Paul writes, "The Son is the image of the invisible God. He existed before anything was created, and he holds all things together" (Colossians 1:15–17, NLT). John's Gospel reinforces this truth: "In the beginning the Word already existed. The Word was with God, and the Word was God. He existed in the beginning with God. God created everything through him, and nothing was created except through him" (John 1:1–3, NLT).

Lucifer, later called Satan, was a created being, a powerful angel who rebelled against God. Scripture affirms this: "How you have fallen from heaven, morning star, son of the dawn! You have been cast down to the earth, you who once laid low the nations!" (Isaiah 14:12, NLT) and "You were the seal of perfection, full of wisdom and perfect in beauty, but you became corrupt because of your splendor" (Ezekiel 28:12–17, NLT). Satan is a real spiritual adversary, actively opposing God and His plan, but he is not divine.

Jesus alone is eternal, the uncreated High Priest, and the Savior of humanity (Hebrews 7:24–25, NLT). Therefore, the Bible never presents Satan as Jesus's brother. Christians are called to faith in Christ's completed work: "Faith shows the reality of what we hope for; it is the evidence of things we cannot see" (Hebrews 11:1, NLT). Believers are assured victory over Satan: "For we do not wrestle against flesh and blood, but against the rulers, against the authorities, against the cosmic powers over this present darkness, against the spiritual forces of evil in the heavenly places" (Ephesians 6:12, NLT). The enemy "comes to steal, kill, and destroy" (John 10:10, NLT) and roams "like a roaring lion, seeking whom he may devour" (1 Peter 5:8, NLT). Yet Christians are more than conquerors through Christ: "No, in all these things we are more than conquerors through him who loved us" (Romans 8:37, NLT).

Faith in Christianity is rooted in God's unchanging love, grace, and sovereignty. Believers do not rely on human authority or ritual but trust in Christ's power and the sufficiency of His Word: "Truly I tell you, heaven and earth will pass away, but my words will never pass away" (Matthew 24:35, NLT). God's Word is final, and His plan of salvation is complete in Jesus Christ.

The Bible presents Satan as a fallen angel who rebelled against God out of pride. He is called "the father of lies" (John 8:44, NLT) and "the accuser of our brothers and sisters" (Revelation 12:10, NLT). Satan's purpose is clear, "The thief's purpose is to steal and kill and destroy" (John 10:10, NLT). He twists God's Word, deceives hearts, and blinds unbelievers to the truth (2 Corinthians 4:4, NLT).

Yet, Satan's power is limited. He cannot act beyond what God permits, as seen in Job's story (Job 1:12, NLT). Scripture warns believers to stay alert, "for your great enemy, the devil, prowls around like a roaring lion, looking for someone to devour" (1 Peter 5:8, NLT). But Christians are not helpless, through Christ, they are "more than conquerors" (Romans 8:37, NLT).

The Bible never portrays Satan as equal to Jesus or as His brother. He is a created being, utterly defeated through the cross. Believers resist him not through ritual or rule but through faith in Christ, the indwelling Holy Spirit, and the authority of God's Word (Ephesians 6:10–11, NLT).

MORMONISM

In *Mormonism*, Satan is also described as a liar and deceiver, yet his portrayal differs sharply from the biblical account. LDS teachings identify him as Lucifer, a spirit <u>brother</u> of Jesus Christ in the premortal realm who rebelled against God's plan of agency (*Moses 4:3; Doctrine and Covenants 29:36–37*). His rebellion is said to have led to the loss of his heavenly standing and the corruption of others.

Modern LDS leaders often teach that "Satan's greatest work is to tear apart the family" and that "*he desires all men to be miserable like unto himself*" (*2 Nephi 2:27*). In Mormon culture and temple ceremony depictions, Satan is sometimes portrayed as cunning and persuasive, an almost friendly manipulator, and in others, as powerless or pitiful.

Satan's supposed influence appears subtly in LDS practices that place barriers between God and His people: the temple veil is reintroduced, and only the Mormon prophet is said to commune with God in the Holy of Holies. False restrictions, such as dietary laws against coffee or tea, are enforced as spiritual obligations rather than matters of conscience. Teachings that children are "perfect until age eight" oppose Scripture's teaching that "all have sinned and fall short of the glory of God" (Romans 3:23, NLT).

This version of Satan diverts attention away from Christ's finished work and toward human systems of worthiness and ritual. By redefining sin, twisting Scripture, and binding members to performance-based salvation, the enemy's deception continues, hidden in religious language.

RELIGION

Jesus never came to start a religion. He came to bring relationship. The Pharisees constantly criticized Him for "breaking" their man-made rules, healing on the Sabbath, walking through grain fields, and even allowing His disciples to eat without washing their hands (Matthew 12:1–14, NLT; Mark 7:1–8, NLT). Jesus rebuked their hypocrisy, saying, "These people honor me with their lips, but their hearts are far from me. Their worship is a farce, for they teach man-made ideas as commands from God" (Mark 7:6–7, NLT).

Religion focuses on performance. Jesus focuses on the heart. God looks beyond appearances: "People judge by outward appearance, but the Lord looks at the heart" (1 Samuel 16:7, NLT).

When Nicodemus approached Jesus at night, Jesus told him plainly that salvation comes only by spiritual rebirth: "Humans can reproduce only human life, but the Holy Spirit gives birth to spiritual life" (John 3:6, NLT). "The wind blows wherever it wants. Just as you can hear the wind but can't tell where it comes from or where it is going, so you can't explain how people are born of the Spirit" (John 3:8, NLT).

True followers of Christ are born again by grace, not by ritual or religious effort. "God saved you by his grace when you believed. And you can't take credit for this; it is a gift from God. Salvation is not a reward for the good things we have done" (Ephesians 2:8–9, NLT).

Jesus's first miracle, turning water into wine (John 2:1–11, NLT), was not to break a rule but to reveal His glory. He later said, "The Son of Man is Lord, even over the Sabbath!" (Matthew 12:8, NLT). In other words, Jesus is greater than religion. He fulfills the law (Matthew 5:17). He invites believers into freedom, not fear, because "where the Spirit of the Lord is, there is freedom" (2 Corinthians 3:17, NLT).

Grace doesn't give us license to sin; it gives us power to overcome sin. Those who live by the Spirit don't need extra rules to prove devotion. They walk in the freedom of Christ's finished work on the cross.

MORMONISM

In *Mormonism*, religion is not viewed as a hindrance but as a divine structure. Members are taught to keep the Sabbath by strict observance, no sports, work, or recreation, as a sign of obedience (Doctrine and Covenants 59:9–13). The LDS Church ties worthiness to rule-keeping, such as abstaining from coffee or tea (Doctrine and Covenants 89:9) and fulfilling callings within the church.

Mormons are encouraged to *"doubt their doubts before they doubt their faith" (Uchtdorf, 2013, General Conference)*, meaning faith is measured by loyalty to the organization rather than personal revelation through Scripture alone. The system emphasizes outward conformity and worthiness interviews rather than inward transformation by grace.

Unlike the Bible, which teaches that salvation is a free gift through faith (Ephesians 2:8–9), Mormon doctrine combines grace and works: *"For we know that it is by grace that we are saved, after all we can do" (2 Nephi*

25:23, Book of Mormon). This makes grace conditional, not free.

In the LDS view, Jesus's atonement opens the door for exaltation, but humans must climb through it by obedience to temple ordinances and covenants. This redefines grace into performance-based religion, the very system Jesus opposed.

Religion in Mormonism is praised; religion in the Bible is exposed. Jesus called out religious hypocrisy, but Mormonism calls it holiness. Christianity says, "It is finished" (John 19:30, NLT). Mormonism says, "There is still more to do."

True Christianity rests in relationship, not religion. Jesus tore the veil. Mormonism sews it back up.

GOD'S VOICE

CHRISTIANITY

When we become Christians, we enter the spiritual realm. Life is no longer guided by what we see or feel, but by the invisible will of God. "For we live by believing and not by seeing" (2 Corinthians 5:7, NLT). The Holy Spirit makes His home in us, teaching, comforting, and speaking as we grow in grace (2 Peter 3:18).

From the beginning, God has spoken to His people. He spoke to Joseph and Jacob through dreams, to Pharaoh and Nebuchadnezzar through signs that required interpretation, and to His prophets through visions. God does not change (Malachi 3:6). Jesus confirmed this truth when He said, "My sheep listen to my voice; I know them, and they follow me" (John 10:27, NLT).

Every believer has been given the right to hear God's voice. When Jesus died, "the curtain in the sanctuary was torn in two" (Luke 23:45, NLT), symbolizing direct access to the Father. God is not silent; He speaks through His Word, His Spirit, and His people. We are a royal priesthood (1 Peter 2:9), chosen to carry His presence wherever we go.

Hearing from God is not for a select few, it's the privilege of all His children. Would a loving Father refuse to speak to His own? Never. The Holy Spirit still leads, still convicts, still whispers truth into the hearts of believers. "The Spirit Himself testifies with our spirit that we are God's children" (Romans 8:16, NLT).

When you hear His voice, test it by Scripture and by peace (1 John 4:1; Colossians 3:15). God will never contradict His written Word. He still heals, still saves, and still speaks to every believer who is willing to listen. Christian believers are cautioned to Matthew 7:15-16 NLT "beware of false prophets who come disguised as harmless sheep but are really vicious wolves. You can identify them by their fruit, that is, by the way they act."

MORMONISM

The Mormons (LDS) teaches that God also speaks, but their system limits revelation primarily to those holding priesthood authority at the top of the Church. According to Mormon scripture *Doctrine and Covenants 1:38, "Whether by mine own voice or by the voice of my servants, it is the same."* This means that revelation to guide the church as a whole must come through the Prophet of the LDS Church and the Quorum of the Twelve Apostles (sometimes the seventy, which are under the twelve).

In *Mormon* belief, members are encouraged to receive personal inspiration for their own lives, but not revelation that would guide or correct the Church. Teachings emphasize that only the Prophet can speak for God to the world. *The Family: A Proclamation to the World (1995) declares, "We, the First Presidency and the Council of the Twelve Apostles… solemnly proclaim…"*—demonstrating that divine guidance flows through those specific offices.

While the Bible teaches that every believer is a priest who can hear God (1 Peter 2:9), the LDS system establishes a spiritual hierarchy. Revelation that contradicts church leadership is considered false or from the wrong source. Members are taught to align their personal impressions with what has already been revealed through the Prophet.

In contrast to the biblical declaration "It is finished" (John 19:30, NLT), LDS teachings describe ongoing covenants, ordinances, and temple rites necessary for exaltation (*Doctrine and Covenants 132*). The *LDS* concept of revelation therefore serves to maintain and expand these ordinances through continuing prophets rather than affirming the once-for-all work of Christ.

The biblical view declares that Christ's atonement was complete, granting all believers direct access to God through the torn veil. The *LDS view* maintains that access to the fullness of God's presence is achieved through church authority, priesthood ordinances, and obedience to continuing revelation.

In essence, biblical Christianity teaches that God's voice is personal and immediate, available to all who are born of the Spirit. *Mormonism* teaches that God's voice is institutional and mediated, available through a prophetic structure.

MODESTY

In the Bible, Jesus warned about people who outwardly display religion but inwardly lack true righteousness. The Pharisees made their garments longer to appear holy before others. Jesus said, "Everything they do is for show. On their arms they wear extra wide prayer boxes with Scripture verses inside, and they wear robes with extra-long tassels" (Matthew 23:5, NLT).

God never intended clothing to be a symbol of spiritual protection. Righteousness does not come from fabric or religious symbols, it comes only through faith in Christ. Jesus said, "I am the way, the truth, and the life. No one can come to the Father except through me" (John 14:6, NLT).

The Bible teaches that no one's righteousness can meet God's standard except through Jesus. "But I warn you—unless your righteousness is better than the righteousness of the teachers of religious law and the Pharisees, you will never enter the Kingdom of Heaven!" (Matthew 5:20, NLT).

True protection comes from the Lord Himself, not from garments or charms. The psalmist wrote, "The Lord is my rock, my fortress, and my savior; my God is my rock, in whom I find protection" (Psalm 18:2, NLT).

God sees beyond what people wear. "People judge by outward appearance, but the Lord looks at the heart" (1 Samuel 16:7, NLT). While Christians are called to dress modestly and with self-respect, our clothing does not determine our holiness, our hearts and actions do. As believers mature, we desire to honor God in how we live and present ourselves. Modesty is not a law; it's an expression of love and wisdom in a world that often lacks both.

MORMONISM

In contrast, the *Mormons* (LDS) teaches that wearing "sacred garments" is an essential expression of covenant faithfulness. According to official LDS sources, garments are described as *"an outward expression of an inward commitment to follow the Savior" (The Church of Jesus Christ of Latter-day Saints, n.d.)*. Members are instructed to wear them daily as a constant reminder of temple covenants and a symbol of divine protection.

LDS stories and teachings often recount even physical protection attributed to these garments, such as bullets or knives being stopped before harming a wearer. The garments have evolved over time, from full-length underclothes reaching wrists and ankles to modern styles and tank tops adapted to cultural norms.

In Mormonism, the belief that garments offer literal, physical protection reflects a misunderstanding of God's power. In biblical teaching, assigning spiritual or protective power to a physical object can cross into superstition or even idolatry. Scripture teaches that protection, righteousness, and holiness come through the Spirit of God, not manmade coverings.

The Christian's security is not in clothing, ritual, or outward signs, but in Christ's finished work. The righteousness that covers us is His righteousness alone.

1 Corinthians 1:18 NLT "The message of the cross is foolish to those who are headed for destruction! But we who are being saved know it is the very power of God."

OLD TESTAMENT

The Old Testament reveals Christ in shadows and prophecy, while the New Testament reveals Him in fulfillment. The Old Testament shows humanity's separation from God through sin, and the New Testament shows reconciliation through Christ. As Jeremiah prophesied,

> "The day is coming," says the Lord, "when I will make a new covenant with the people of Israel and Judah… I will put my instructions deep within them, and I will write them on their hearts. I will be their God, and they will be my people" (Jeremiah 31:31–33, NLT).

This covenant points directly to Jesus Christ, who fulfilled every law and sacrifice. Humanity could not earn salvation through obedience; it is a gift of grace. Jesus said,

> "Don't misunderstand why I have come. I did not come to abolish the law of Moses or the writings of the prophets. No, I came to accomplish their purpose" (Matthew 5:17, NLT).

In Genesis, man was cut off from God's presence. In Revelation, God restores that relationship: no more curse, no more tears (Revelation 21:4). Christ reversed the curse of Adam through His finished work on the cross.

> "For as in Adam all die, so also in Christ shall all be made alive" (1 Corinthians 15:22, NLT).

Salvation is not achieved through human effort, ritual, or obedience to law—but through Christ's righteousness alone. Jesus is the second Adam who restores what was lost (Romans 5:17–19). His words in the Sermon on the Mount ("You have heard it said…but I say…") revealed the heart of God's law, showing that righteousness is inward, not merely outward.

MORMONISM

Mormonism acknowledges the Old Testament but continues to uphold Old Testament–style laws and ordinances as necessary for righteousness. The LDS faith teaches that obedience to laws and temple covenants is required for exaltation (Doctrine and Covenants 130:20–21). While the Bible teaches that the New Covenant replaces the old, Mormon doctrine often merges the two, emphasizing human participation in earning God's favor.

The Book of Mormon also teaches that Christ's atonement applies only after the *"age of accountability"*, usually age eight (*Moroni 8:10–12*), *implying* that salvation is conditional upon human decision and obedience. In contrast, Scripture teaches that salvation is fully accomplished through Christ's finished work on the cross, not dependent on human maturity or effort.

While the Bible proclaims "It is finished" (John 19:30), *Mormonism* teaches that perfection is attainable through obedience to temple ordinances and covenants (*Doctrine and Covenants 1:31–32*). This mindset reintroduces the very law Christ fulfilled, minimizing the sufficiency of His sacrifice.

BIBLICALLY, The Old Testament points to Jesus; the New Testament fulfills Him. The law exposes sin, but grace brings redemption. Christianity rests on the truth that Jesus alone is enough. *Mormonism,* though honoring Scripture in part, continues to add requirements Christ already completed. The difference is simple yet eternal: law or grace, self-effort or Christ's finished work.

AUTHORITY

CHRISTIANITY

The believer's authority begins with union with Christ. When God abides in you, His Spirit empowers you, strengthens you, teaches you, and gives you the boldness to walk in what He has called you to do. Authority is not something you earn, it is something you receive, male or female, because you belong to Jesus.

Jesus Himself said:

> "Anyone who believes in me will do the <u>same works</u> I have done, and even greater works… You can ask for anything in my name, and I will do it… He is the Holy Spirit, who leads into all truth"
> (John 14:12–17, NLT)

This means believers operate under Christ's authority, not their own. We are seated with Him (Eph. 2:6). Our names are written in heaven (Luke 10:20). He finishes the work He begins:

> "God… will continue his work until it is finally finished"
> (Phil. 1:6, NLT)

Understanding Scripture does not come from reading alone, but from the Spirit opening the heart. When spiritual understanding feels blocked, Paul explains that:

> "Satan… has blinded the minds of those who don't believe"
> (2 Cor. 4:3–4, NLT)

But when the veil is lifted, God's Word flows like a river, illuminating, clarifying, healing, and transforming. These moments do not change God's love for us; they simply deepen our love for Him.

Authority is always exercised in Jesus' name alone (John 14:14). God uses willing vessels, but the power belongs entirely to Him (Prov. 16:4). As Christ lives through us, we become new creations (2 Cor. 5:17). Paul says it simply:

> "It is no longer I who live, but Christ lives in me… I do not treat the grace of God as meaningless."
> (Gal. 2:20–21, NLT)

God does not forget His children or their labor:

> "God is not unjust. He will not forget how hard you have worked for him."
> (Heb. 6:10, NLT)

"…for you are a chosen people. You are royal priests, a holy nation, God's very own possession. As a result, you can show others the goodness of God, for he called you out of the darkness into his wonderful light." (1 Peter 2:9 NLT)

In Conclusion, the Jesus believer's authority is this: Christ in you.Christ working through you. Christ receiving the glory. Faith is what He asks. He supplies the rest.

MORMONISM

Mormon LDS teaching states that spiritual authority comes through two priesthood lines, Aaronic and Melchizedek:

> *"The Melchizedek Priesthood holds the right of presidency, and has power and authority over all the offices in the church."*
> *(Doctrine and Covenants 107:8)*

According to *Mormon LDS* doctrine, you cannot act in God's name unless you hold LDS priesthood authority.

> *"Priesthood authority is required to perform ordinances… and to preside in the Church."*
> *(Official LDS Manual, Cht 14 "Priesthood Organization")*

The Mormon LDS Church also teach that priesthood power increases with righteousness:

> *"That the rights of the priesthood are inseparably connected with the powers of heaven… only upon the principles of righteousness."*
> *(Doctrine and Covenants 121:36)*

If a priesthood holder is "unworthy," his authority and power are revoked.

> *"The heavens withdraw themselves… Amen to the priesthood or the authority of that man."*
> *(Doctrine and Covenants 121:37)*

VEIL

CHRISTIANITY

In 2 Corinthians 3:14–16 (NLT), Paul teaches that the people of Moses's time were blinded by a veil over their hearts:

"But the people's minds were hardened, and to this day whenever the old covenant is being read, the same veil covers their minds so they cannot understand the truth. And this veil can be removed only by believing in Christ. Yes, even today when they read Moses' writings, their hearts are covered with that veil, and they do not understand. But whenever someone turns to the Lord, the veil is taken away."

The "veil" represents spiritual blindness, an inability to see God's truth clearly. Through Jesus Christ, that barrier has been removed. When He cried out on the cross, "It is finished" (John 19:30, NLT), the veil in the temple was torn in two (Matthew 27:51, NLT), symbolizing that access to God was now open for all believers.

In Christ, every believer can speak to God directly. Scripture affirms that there is "one God and one Mediator who can reconcile God and humanity, the man Christ Jesus" (1 Timothy 2:5, NLT). Pastors and teachers exist to equip the saints (Ephesians 4:11–12, NLT), but they do not serve as mediators between God and man. The true church is not a building or an institution but the living body of

Christ, the believers themselves (1 Corinthians 12:27, NLT).

Because the veil is already torn, Christians live in the light of direct fellowship with God through the Spirit. No temple structure or human priesthood is needed to approach His presence.

MORMONISM

In *Mormon Latter-day Saint (LDS)* temples, a literal veil remains central to temple ceremonies. According to Doctrine and Covenants 101:23 and temple instruction manuals, the veil represents separation between mortals and God, to be lifted at the Second Coming. This teaching implies that full access to God's presence has not yet been granted.

The Book of Mormon and Doctrine and Covenants also emphasize continuing mediators through modern prophets and apostles. The LDS Church teaches that the living prophet and the Quorum of the Twelve Apostles act as God's authorized mouthpieces on earth (*Doctrine and Covenants 107:22–23*). In practice, members receive divine guidance through these appointed mediators and local bishops.

By contrast, biblical Christianity teaches that Jesus alone fulfills this role completely. The LDS continuation of temple veils and hierarchical mediators places a barrier where the New Covenant declares none.

MARRIAGE

CHRISTIANITY

Jesus' teaching on marriage in eternity is direct and unmistakable. When questioned about a woman who had been married to seven brothers, Jesus responded, "For when the dead rise, they will neither marry nor be given in marriage. In this respect they will be like the angels in heaven" (Matthew 22:30, NLT). Marriage is God-ordained, but it is for this life, not the resurrection.

Jesus continues by reminding the crowds that God is "the God of the living, not the dead" (Matthew 22:32, NLT). Earthly relationships, including marriage, are temporary. Eternal life is rooted in knowing Christ, not in earthly institutions (John 17:3).

MORMONISM

Mormonism often cites Matthew 18:18 ("whatever you bind on earth shall be bound in heaven") to justify eternal marriage. But in context, Jesus is speaking about church discipline and reconciliation between believers (Matthew 18:15–18, NLT). This particular verse has nothing to do with marriage sealing or temple ordinances.

LDS doctrine teaches that reaching "exaltation" (the highest heaven, to become a god) requires temple marriage. In other words, salvation to the "top tier" depends on being sealed in marriage here on earth AND in heaven.

The *Mormon LDS* Church teaches that marriage and procreation (having babies) continues after death and that couples must be sealed in a temple to reach the highest level of heaven. *Doctrine and Covenants* states that a man and woman married "by my word" will remain sealed for eternity (*D&C 132:19*). *The Family: A Proclamation to the World declares that families can be "sealed" forever and that eternal marriage is central to exaltation.*

When Jesus says one thing and a religious system says another, the believer must decide whose words are true. Jesus or Joseph?

NEW TESTAMENT

CHRISTIANITY

The New Testament announces that everything the Old Covenant pointed to is fulfilled in Jesus Christ. The tabernacle, priesthood, sacrifices, and ritual washings all prepared the way for something greater, Christ's once-for-all work on the cross.

Hebrews explains this clearly: the high priest entered the holy place yearly with blood for himself and the people, showing "that the way into the Most Holy Place was not yet open" (Hebrews 9:8, NLT). These rituals were "temporary provisions" until the time God appointed for reformation.

But then the true High Priest came:

"So Christ has now become the High Priest over all the good things that have come… With his own blood, not the blood of goats and calves, he entered the Most Holy Place once for all time and secured our redemption forever." (Hebrews 9:11–12, NLT)

This is past tense. He did it. Christ's work is finished. Salvation is complete. The believer does not add to Christ, he trusts Christ. The old is gone; the new has come.

Jesus told Martha, "I am the resurrection and the life. Anyone who believes in me will live, even after dying." (John 11:25, NLT).

In Him, the fear of death loses its power. Eternal life begins now because Christ Himself is our life.

Jesus gave a picture of the New Covenant when He said:

"No one puts new wine into old wineskins… New wine calls for new wineskins." (Mark 2:22, NLT).

You cannot pour grace into a system built on works. The gospel is not an upgrade to the Old Testament, it is the <u>completion</u> of it. The Old Covenant is "old" precisely because it has been fulfilled. You don't cling to an old garment or drink from an old wineskin when the new has come.

Paul said it plainly: everything he once trusted in, genealogy, status, works, was "garbage" compared to knowing Christ (Philippians 3:8, NLT). The New Testament does not invite us to improve ourselves but to surrender ourselves to the <u>finished work of Jesus</u>.

MORMONISM

Mormon LDS teachings present a system that blends Old Testament patterns with new requirements Joseph Smith introduced, creating a hybrid that the Bible does not support. The New Testament declares the old covenant fulfilled and set aside. Mormon doctrine <u>revives</u> it, elements including: a standing Aaronic priesthood, temple rituals, ceremonial washings, genealogical requirements, the veil, and worthiness-based access to God.

Mormon doctrine, Doctrine and Covenants 13 claims the Aaronic Priesthood was restored by John the Baptist and is necessary for baptisms and *"the ministering of angels."* Yet Hebrews teaches that the Aaronic priesthood was temporary and replaced by Christ's eternal priesthood.

The Book of Mormon teaches that salvation comes "after all we can do" (2 Nephi 25:23). LDS scripture also teaches that weakness becomes strength only "after the trial of your faith" (Ether 12:27). This framework makes righteousness dependent on human effort.

Mormonism emphasizes the stories of the New Testament, emphasizing holidays like Christmas and Easter, while ignoring its core message: the old is gone, the new has come. LDS teaching retains the veil, temple ordinances, genealogical requirements, and priesthood systems, all of which the New Testament says **<u>Christ fulfilled</u>** (see Matthew 5:17; Romans 10:4; Hebrews 10:1-10; Hebrews 9:12; Hebrews 7:11-12; Hebrews 7:24-25; Colossians 2:13-14; Ephesians 2:14-15; Colossians 2:16-17; Hebrews 8:5).

To keep both the old and the new is to burst the wineskin. Jesus will not be patched onto a system of self-righteousness. Grace cannot be mixed with works.

MEN

CHRISTIANITY

Biblical manhood begins not with cultural expectations but with God Himself. Scripture presents manhood as a calling rooted in humility, repentance, and reliance on the Lord. A man is first a worshiper before he is a leader. The psalmist writes, "The righteous man walks with integrity; blessed are his children who follow him" (Prov. 20:7, NLT). Biblical manhood is grounded in character, not performance.

A Christian man submits his life to God, recognizing that he is created, dependent, and accountable. Scripture affirms that men and women alike are made in God's image (Gen. 1:27, NLT), yet men hold distinct responsibilities within the home and church. These responsibilities are not a hierarchy of value but a structure designed by God for flourishing. Paul describes the husband's leadership as sacrificial and self-giving, modeled after Christ Himself: "For husbands, this means love your wives, just as Christ loved the church. He gave up his life for her" (Eph. 5:25, NLT).

Christian manhood centers on humility before God, mastery over one's desires, faithful provision, protective strength, and spiritual leadership. These traits reflect a heart transformed by Christ rather than shaped by societal expectations. Jesus teaches that true greatness is found in servanthood, not status (Mark 10:43–45, NLT). Thus, biblical manhood does not pursue glory for self but points all honor back to God.

Christian men do not strive to be saviors or compete for spiritual rank. Scripture is clear: "There is one God and one Mediator who can reconcile God and humanity—the man Christ Jesus" (1 Tim. 2:5, NLT). A biblical man lives as a servant under God's authority, not as a god in embryo.

MORMONISM

Mormon Latter-day Saint doctrine frames manhood within an eternal progression in which men can advance to godhood. According to LDS teaching, faithful Mormon men may become exalted and inherit divine status, ruling worlds in eternity. The Doctrine and Covenants states that those who receive exaltation *"shall be gods" (D&C 132:20)*. Rather than emphasizing human dependence on God, LDS theology elevates worthy men toward becoming like God in essence, not merely in character.

This system inevitably shapes the expectations placed on Mormon men. Their worthiness, authority, and leadership are tied to performance within the church structure. The Family Proclamation declares that fathers are to "preside" with righteousness and maintain "providing" and "protecting" roles, but these responsibilities are often paired with the pressure to achieve spiritual advancement, maintain flawless outward behavior, and conform to institutional expectations. Masculinity is measured not only by character but by visible worthiness, priesthood advancement, and adherence to prescribed duties.

In contrast to biblical teaching, which places glory and saviorhood solely on Christ, LDS doctrine speaks of men acting as proxy saviors through ordinances for the dead *(D&C 128:18)* and progressing toward exaltation by obedience to laws and ordinances *(3 Nephi 27:19)*. While

Christian manhood bows <u>low</u> before God, Mormon manhood is taught to advance upward toward becoming like God in nature.

The result is a fundamentally different vision: the Bible calls men to humility, service, and Christ-centered leadership, while Mormonism frames manhood within a ladder of worthiness and eternal ascent. Scripture teaches dependence; LDS teaching promotes progression. The Christian man trusts in the finished work of Christ. The Mormon man strives toward godhood.

DEATH

Christians believe that when a person dies, their soul immediately faces judgment before God. Scripture says, "And just as each person is destined to die once and after that comes judgment" (Hebrews 9:27, NLT). There is no delay, no waiting place, and no second chance. The moment death occurs, the eternal destination, Heaven or Hell, is sealed.

Jesus described this vividly in the parable of the rich man and Lazarus: "The rich man also died and was buried, and he went to the place of the dead. There, in torment, he saw Abraham in the far distance with Lazarus at his side" (Luke 16:22–23, NLT). The rich man immediately found himself in anguish, aware of his separation from God, and begged that someone would warn his brothers. Yet Abraham answered that those who reject the truth already revealed through Scripture would not believe even if someone rose from the dead (Luke 16:31).

This understanding produces urgency in the believer's heart—to live rightly before God, to love others deeply, and to share the gospel boldly. Because judgment follows immediately after death, Christians know that now is the time to repent, to pray, and to lead others to Jesus. As Paul wrote, "Indeed, the 'right time' is now. Today is the day of salvation" (2 Corinthians 6:2, NLT).

MORMONISM

In contrast, *Mormon* doctrine teaches that after death, souls enter a temporary state known as Spirit Paradise or Spirit Prison (*Book of Mormon, Alma 40:11–14; Doctrine and Covenants 138:10–22*). The righteous wait peacefully in Paradise, while others remain in Spirit Prison, where they can still learn, repent, and accept the gospel. This "spirit world" exists before the final judgment and resurrection.

Mormons believe that temple ordinances and proxy baptisms performed on earth can benefit those who have died, giving them further chances for exaltation (*Doctrine and Covenants 138:57–59*). Final judgment, according to LDS teaching, comes later, after these opportunities are completed.

This view removes the biblical immediacy of judgment. While Christians see death as the point of no return, Mormonism presents it as a stage for continued progress and potential redemption. The difference shapes how each faith approaches life on earth: for believers in Christ, time is precious because eternity begins the moment we die; for Latter-day Saints, death opens another chapter of ongoing opportunity.

One faith calls for urgency, the other allows delay. The Bible teaches that now is the time to choose Christ. Eternity begins the moment we take our last breath.

INTERVIEW QUESTIONS

CHRISTIANITY

Scripture presents a God who saves sinners by grace rather than by a lifetime of religious performance. Jesus calls His people to come to Him with honesty, not perfection. The gospel does not demand a long list of worthiness proofs. It requires one thing: faith in Christ alone. "Believe in the Lord Jesus and you will be saved" (Acts 16:31, NLT).

Paul emphasizes that salvation is God's work, not ours: "God saved you by his grace when you believed. And you can't take credit for this; it is a gift from God. Salvation is not a reward for the good things we have done" (Ephesians 2:8–9, NLT). Because Christ fulfilled the law perfectly, believers rest in His righteousness rather than their own (2 Corinthians 5:21, NLT).

Christian hope is rooted in the finished work of Jesus, not in a lifelong attempt to prove worthiness. This creates a life marked by freedom, honesty, and peace. "Where the Spirit of the Lord is, there is freedom" (2 Corinthians 3:17, NLT).

Biblical Christianity does not require an interview to determine one's spiritual standing. The condition for entering God's presence is simply this: trust in Christ as Lord and Savior. The gospel produces humility, not performance-driven anxiety; rest, not pressure to appear perfect; and confidence in Christ's work, rather than fear of personal inadequacy.

MORMONISM

Mormon Latter-day Saint doctrine places temple entrance, and the possibility of exaltation, on the basis of personal worthiness, obedience, and loyalty to the Church. Entrance into the temple is determined not by faith alone, but by successfully answering a series of interview questions. These questions are considered essential because, according to LDS teaching, the temple is the place where saving ordinances for exaltation occur (*Doctrine and Covenants 131:1–4*).

The pressure created by these expectations has been widely noted in Utah culture. High depression rates and the "perfection lifestyle" are often connected to the burden of projecting spiritual and social flawlessness. Members are encouraged to appear successful, morally spotless, and ever-cheerful. Even those with modest incomes may enter multimillion-dollar temples if they are deemed worthy, pay a full tithe, and provide acceptable answers in the interview.

<u>Here are some temple interview questions issued to LDS members:</u>

Do you have a testimony of the Atonement of Jesus Christ and of His role as your Savior and Redeemer?

Do you have a testimony of the **Restoration (Joseph Smith)** of the gospel of Jesus Christ?

Do you *sustain (a fancy word for "bow down to")* the President of the Church of Jesus Christ of Latter-Day Saints as the prophet, seer, and revelator and as the only person on the earth authorized to exercise all priesthood keys?

Do you *sustain* the members of the First Presidency and the Quorum of the Twelve Apostles as prophets, seers, and revelators?

Do you *sustain* the other General Authorities and local leaders of the Church?

The Lord has said that all things are to be "done in cleanliness" before Him (D&C 42:41).

Do you strive for moral cleanliness in your thoughts and behavior?

Do you obey the law of chastity?

Do you follow the teachings of the Church of Jesus Christ in your private and public behavior with members of your family and others?

Do you support or promote any teachings, practices, or doctrine contrary to those of the Church?

Do you strive to keep the Sabbath Day holy, both at home and at church; attend your meetings; prepare for and worthily partake of the sacrament; and live your life in harmony with the laws and commandments of the gospel?

<u>Are you a full tithe payer?</u>

For new members seeking a limited-use recommend: Are you willing to obey the commandment to pay tithing?

Do you understand and obey the Word of Wisdom? (no coffee, no tea, no strong drink)

Do you have any financial or other obligations to a former spouse or to children? If yes, are you current in meeting those obligations?

Do you keep the covenants that you made in the temple, including wearing the temple garment as instructed in the endowment?

Are there serious sins in your life that need to be resolved with priesthood authorities as part of your repentance?

Do you consider yourself worthy to enter the Lord's house and participate in temple ordinances?

In *Mormon LDS* doctrine, these questions and more determine access to ordinances that lead to exaltation.

 In biblical Christianity, access to God rests on Christ alone. Thus, the two systems stand in direct contrast. One calls the believer to trust in the finished work of Jesus. The other requires demonstrated worthiness through sustained obedience. One offers rest for weary souls. The other produces an ongoing struggle to measure up.

TEMPLE CEREMONY

CHRISTIANITY

In Old Testament times, the temple served as a sacred place where priests offered animal sacrifices on behalf of the people. The priest entered the Holy of Holies alone, symbolizing the separation between a holy God and sinful humanity. According to Leviticus 16:2–3 (NLT), only the high priest could enter once a year with the blood of an animal sacrifice.

Jewish tradition tells that a cord was tied around the priest's ankle as he entered, in case he died in God's presence and had to be pulled out. This illustrates the seriousness of approaching God without atonement. Each sacrifice pointed forward to the ultimate sacrifice, Jesus Christ, the Lamb of God.

When Jesus died, "the curtain in the sanctuary of the Temple was torn in two, from top to bottom" (Matthew 27:51, NLT). This tearing of the veil signified that through Christ's blood, direct access to God was now open to all who believe. The book of Hebrews explains that "by his death, Jesus opened a new and life-giving way through the curtain into the Most Holy Place" (Hebrews 10:19–20, NLT).

The Old Covenant rituals were a foreshadow, temporary symbols pointing to the finished work of Christ. Under the New Covenant, no animal sacrifice, temple ceremony, or human priesthood is needed for atonement. Jesus fulfilled it all.

While biblical faith teaches that believers now have direct access to God through Jesus alone, the LDS temple reintroduces ceremony, mediators, and ritual progression. This restores the separation that the torn veil declared finished.

The Bible teaches that "by <u>ONE</u> offering he forever made perfect those who are being made holy" (Hebrews 10:14, NLT). Salvation is not obtained through temple rites but through faith in the finished sacrifice of Jesus Christ.

MORMONISM

In the *Mormon LDS* temple ceremony, rituals continue to reenact symbolic acts and covenants, including ceremonial clothing, signs, and oaths said to represent entry into God's presence. These practices are viewed as sacred ordinances required for exaltation (see Doctrine and Covenants 124:39–41). The temple system in Mormonism mirrors Old Testament symbolism, rituals, garments, and a restricted temple space, rather than recognizing that Christ's atonement has already opened the way.

During *Mormon* temple ceremonies, participants are instructed never to reveal or demonstrate the token signs or hand gestures learned within the temple. These rituals closely resemble Masonic practices and incorporate selected phrases drawn from the Bible.

After the instructional presentation concludes, temple participants approach what is called "the veil". There, they speak with another Mormon temple worker positioned on the opposite side. The individual at the veil tests the participant's knowledge through a series of questions that must be answered correctly using specific hand gestures and phrases. These questions and gestures are presented as being connected to the Aaronic and Melchizedek Priesthood authority.

Some of The final wording in the climax of the Mormon Temple is TAKEN out from the Bible:

Proverbs 3:7-8 "Be not wise in thine own eyes; Fear Jehovah, and depart from evil: It will be health to thy navel, And marrow to thy bones."

The rearranging or rephrasing of Scripture for secret use does not make it sacred; rather, it moves away from the simplicity of the gospel. God's Word warns us not to alter His message: "Do not add to what I command you, and do not subtract from it" (Deuteronomy 4:2, NLT). Scripture is complete and holy as given, adding secret words, gestures, or symbols only obscures the truth rather than revealing it.

Couldn't those same blessings, health and strength, be received through prayer and obedience to God's Word, rather than through secret temple phrases? Scripture shows that faith, not ceremony, brings life to the soul and health to the body.

The contrast is clear: In Christianity, the sacrifice is complete, the blood of Christ once for all. In Mormonism, the rituals continue, implying the atonement's work is not yet fully applied without temple ordinances.

ANGELS

Angels are real, created beings who exist to glorify God and carry out His purposes. Scripture teaches that "through him God created everything... the visible and the invisible" (Colossians 1:16, NLT). Angels are created above man and below God, possessing intellect, will, and moral responsibility. Some remained faithful to God, and others rebelled with Satan (2 Peter 2:4, NLT).

Angels minister to believers: "Therefore, angels are only servants, spirits sent to care for people who will inherit salvation." (Hebrews 1:14, NLT). They speak and act only in perfect alignment with God's Word.

Because of this, every angelic experience must be tested by Scripture. Paul gives his strong warning: "Let God's curse fall on anyone... even an angel from heaven, who preaches a different kind of Good News" (Galatians 1:8, NLT). True angels never contradict the Bible.

Jesus taught that in the resurrection people "will neither marry nor be given in marriage. In this respect they will be like the angels in heaven." (Mark 12:25, NLT). Jesus uses a simile, like the angels, to describe a condition, not a transformation. We, mere humans, do not become angels. We remain human, redeemed, and in Christ we will one day even judge angels (1 Corinthians 6:3, NLT).

Angels also do not experience redemption. Christ died for humanity, not angels. Saved humans will know a song of redeeming love that angels cannot sing.

Scripture reveals both elect angels and fallen ones. Cherubim and Seraphim appear before God (Ezekiel 1:1–27), while fallen angels operate under Satan's destructive purposes. Even in Job, fallen angels must respond to God's authority (Job 1–2). No angel has ever beheld God's full essence.

Encounters with angels do happen, but they must lead us back to Scripture, never away from it. Any message that adds to the Bible or redirects someone from it must be rejected.

MORMONISM

Mormon LDS doctrine teaches ideas about angels that diverge sharply from Scripture. Joseph Smith's teachings reinterpret Jesus' words about angels in a way the Bible does not support.

Mormon Doctrine and Covenants 132:15–17 teaches that people who are not married in a Mormon temple <u>will become angels</u> in the afterlife, remaining single, "ministering servants," and without exaltation. According to Smith, such angels did not *"abide the law"* and therefore cannot progress to godhood.

Mormon Doctrine and Covenants 129 instructs members to test angels by shaking their hands to discern if the being is resurrected, mortal, or demonic. If they feel a hand like a human, they are said to be resurrected. If the hand goes through, they are said to be demonic. (Very interesting when you compare that the Bible says GOD IS SPIRIT.)

Mormon LDS teaching confuses the biblical distinction between humans and angels. Mormons are taught that righteous humans can progress toward godhood, while others become angels as a lesser eternal status. BIBLICAL Scripture teaches humans never become angels and never lose their humanity in the resurrection.

CAREFUL OF SIMILES: Mormon LDS doctrine frequently misinterprets biblical figures of speech, such as two similes: For instance, many LDS teachers insist Jesus literally bled in Gethsemane because Luke says His sweat fell "like drops of blood" (Luke 22:44, NLT). This is a simile, not a medical statement. Second, LDS teachers insist humans will <u>literally</u> become angels in heaven in the afterlife when Jesus says "they will be like the angels in heaven." These misreadings create doctrines the Bible never teaches.

2 Corinthians 11:14 "And no wonder, for even Satan disguises himself as an angel of light."

SALVATION VS. EXALTATION

CHRISTIANITY

Christianity teaches a simple yet profound gospel: there is one God, eternally perfect, who sent His Son, Jesus Christ, to bridge the gap between a holy Creator and fallen humanity. By placing our faith in Christ, His substitutionary death on the cross becomes our hope. "For God so loved the world, that he gave his only Son, that whoever believes in him should not perish but have eternal life" (John 3:16, NLT).

Jesus is our mediator, not another god. The New Testament makes clear: "there is one God and one Mediator who can reconcile God and humanity, the man Christ Jesus" (1 Tim. 2:5, NLT). Through Christ's blood, we are adopted as children of God; we are not destined to become deities ourselves. Our identity in Him is as beloved sons and daughters, heirs of God's kingdom (Romans 8:16–17).

As believers, we receive God's Holy Spirit, who gives us direct access to Him. We do not rely on any human priesthood to speak to God for us. Our relationship is personal, intimate, and grounded in grace.

When the Bible talks about "exalting," it exalts God, not humans. Indeed, Scripture warns against pride and lofty thoughts: "We demolish arguments and every pretension that sets itself up against the knowledge of God, and we take captive every thought to make it obedient to Christ" (2 Cor. 10:5, NLT). Our call is humility, not ascent to divinity.

The book of Revelation paints a glorious promise, but not of humans becoming gods. In the new Jerusalem, "no sun is needed, nor moon, to shine on it, for the glory of God gives it light, and the Lamb is its lamp" (Rev. 21:23, NLT). God Himself is the center; He is the light forever, and we worship Him, not replace Him.

In short, the Christian gospel offers salvation, eternal life with God, not exaltation to godhood. Our purpose is not to become gods, but to glorify the one true God, our Father, forever.

MORMONISM

In contrast, *Mormon* theology centers on a very different goal: *exaltation.* According to LDS teaching, the ultimate aim is not merely to be saved, but to become gods ourselves. This idea is rooted in early Mormon doctrine, particularly in Joseph Smith's famous King Follett Discourse.

Smith taught that "God himself was once as we are now, and is an exalted man" (Smith, 1844/2007, as quoted in Foundations of the Restoration) . He described a path of progress: "by going … from grace to grace, from exaltation to exaltation … until you arrive … at the station of a God" (Smith, 1844/2007) . This is not a peripheral teaching; it is tied to the very notion of eternal life in LDS thought.

Lorenzo Snow, a later LDS president, famously summarized this doctrine in a couplet: *"As man is now, God once was; as God now is, man may become."* According to LDS sources, this is a revelation and a fundamental principle of the faith.

In *Mormon* belief, exaltation is intimately bound up with eternal marriage and temple ordinances. When a man and woman are sealed in the temple, they may inherit *"all heights and depths ... then shall they be gods, because they have no end"* (Smith, cited in BYU-Idaho study guide) . This teaching leads to the belief that exalted couples will govern their own worlds, continue in eternal progression, and participate in an "one eternal round" of creation (Joseph Smith's illustration of the soul's endless capacity) .

Mormon theology thereby asserts many gods, not one. The pathway to divinity is open: faithful men and women may ascend, generation after generation, to sit "in everlasting power" (Smith, 1844/2007) . This is vastly different from the Christian confession of a <u>singular, unchanging God.</u>

From the Christian perspective, the gospel is not about achieving godhood, it is about receiving God's own life, being reconciled through Christ, and dwelling in worship of the one true God forever. By contrast, Mormonism envisions exaltation as a literal ascent to divinity, through eternal marriage and obedience to temple ordinances, based on teachings like Joseph Smith's King Follett Discourse and Lorenzo Snow's couplet.

The heart of Christianity is resting in Christ, not striving to become another god.

ARCHAEOLOGICAL ACCURACY

CHRISTIANITY

Scripture teaches that the Bible is God-breathed and trustworthy: "All Scripture is inspired by God" (2 Timothy 3:16, NLT). The New Testament stands alone among ancient writings in historical reliability. While most ancient books survive through manuscripts copied nearly a thousand years after their original composition, the New Testament has manuscripts dating within decades. With more than 5,700 Greek manuscripts (far surpassing any work of antiquity), the text can be verified with remarkable precision.

Despite being written by over forty authors across fifteen centuries and three continents, the Bible remains unified in message: God's redemptive work in Christ. Its historical claims rest on real geography and archaeology: Jerusalem, Bethlehem, Judea, and countless discovered sites that confirm biblical narratives. Scripture is rooted in the real world because the God who inspired it works in real history. The Bible's preservation reflects His character: faithful, eternal, and unfailing.

MORMONISM

Mormon Latter-day Saint scripture presents an entirely different pattern of origin and preservation. The Book of Mormon has no surviving ancient manuscripts; its existence depends solely on Joseph Smith's 19th-century translation and the claim that the plates were divinely removed. Unlike the Bible's traceable manuscript lineage, the Book of Mormon has no external textual history.

Archaeology further separates the two. Every major biblical location can be placed on a map today, while no Book of Mormon city–Zarahemla, Bountiful, the land of Nephi, has been confirmed anywhere in the world. Official LDS materials acknowledge the lack of identified sites. Where the Bible is anchored in verifiable history, the Book of Mormon remains without archaeological, geographical, or linguistic support.

Christian theology rests on a Scripture that is historically grounded, publicly accessible, and demonstrably preserved. Mormon doctrine relies on a text with no ancient evidence and a narrative detached from the physical record of human history. The contrast underscores a simple truth: the Bible's accuracy and efficacy stand on a foundation God Himself has preserved.

REBUKE

Many believers hesitate to share truth when it conflicts with others' beliefs. Yet Scripture reminds us that love and truth are inseparable. "If I could speak all the languages of earth and of angels, but didn't love others, I would only be a noisy gong or a clanging cymbal" (1 Corinthians 13:1, NLT). True love speaks truth, gently, but boldly, because eternity is at stake.

Jesus Himself never compromised the truth to keep peace. He healed on the Sabbath (Mark 3:1–6), ate with sinners (Matthew 9:10–13), and rebuked hypocrisy (Matthew 23:27). His obedience to God's Word mattered more than man's approval. As followers of Christ, we are called to do the same: "Preach the word of God. Be prepared, whether the time is favorable or not. Patiently correct, rebuke, and encourage your people with good teaching" (2 Timothy 4:2, NLT).

The Great Commission is not optional. Jesus commanded, "Go and make disciples of all the nations, baptizing them… and teaching these new disciples to obey all the commands I have given you" (Matthew 28:19–20, NLT). Sharing the gospel, even when it's uncomfortable, is an act of obedience and love. "For I am not ashamed of this Good News about Christ. It is the power of God at work, saving everyone who believes" (Romans 1:16, NLT).

To love others is not to remain silent. It means caring enough to tell them the truth about salvation, sin, and the Savior. It is not arrogance, it is compassion.

MORMONISM

In *Mormon* culture, open criticism of the Church or its teachings is often seen as offensive or un-Christlike. Many members believe defending their faith means avoiding "contention" and promoting harmony. *The Book of Mormon* teaches that *"the Spirit of the Lord doth not dwell in unholy temples, neither will he dwell in temples of contention" (3 Nephi 11:29)*. Thus, questioning LDS doctrine is frequently labeled as contentious or unloving.

At the same time, Mormonism maintains one of the largest missionary programs in the world. Mormon *Doctrine and Covenants 68:8 commands, "Go ye into all the world, preach the gospel to every creature, acting in the authority which I have given you."* Over seventy thousand full-time missionaries are sent each year to convert others to the LDS faith. The goal, as stated in *Preach My Gospel (2004), is to "invite all to come unto Christ by helping them receive the restored gospel."*

While many Mormons personally avoid online debate, their church's institutional mission is global evangelism, to persuade all people that the LDS Church alone holds the restored truth. This contrasts sharply with biblical Christianity, which proclaims salvation by grace through faith alone (Ephesians 2:8–9), not by joining a specific institution or receiving temple ordinances.

Biblical love is not silence, it's courage with compassion. Jesus spoke truth even when it offended religious leaders. To love someone enough to tell them about the real Jesus is not pride, it's obedience. True disciples do not bow to man's approval; they stand firm in God's Word and proclaim the gospel in love.

EVANGELISM

Now that you've read the contrasts between Mormonism and Christianity, your mind might be doing a few mental gymnastics. (If not, praise God! This must be your calling.)

If you're stepping into evangelizing Mormons, it's vital to understand how they think (see Book 1). I'm deeply grateful that God allowed me to understand that mindset so I could bring truth to others twenty-seven years later.

A. Religious vs. Spiritual

When I was Mormon, being called "religious" felt like a compliment. It meant I was doing my job well, working hard and staying devoted. But as a Christian, when someone calls me "religious," I think, How dare you? Religious people killed Jesus! Works don't get me to heaven. God sent His Son to save us from our sins through the name of Jesus.

Many ex-Mormon atheists or apostates lump all faiths together, as if religion were one giant scoop of vanilla ice cream. They see their new beliefs as colorful and freeing, unaware that this kind of self-made "freedom" leads only to bondage.

Man-made religion always promises growth through effort, but the Bible warns otherwise:

"They will act religious, but they will reject the power that could make them godly. Stay away from people like that!" (2 Timothy 3:5, NLT).

B. The Battle for Truth

If you're witnessing to Mormons, remember, the enemy is strategic. He uses extra "scriptures" to confuse and distort truth. LDS members may quote the Book of Mormon, Doctrine and Covenants, or Pearl of Great Price to defend false revelations.

Yet Scripture stands firm:

- "Beware of false prophets… you will recognize them by their fruits." (Matthew 7:15-16, NLT)
- "If anyone adds to what is written… God will add to that person the plagues described in this book." (Revelation 22:18-19, NLT)
- "All Scripture is inspired by God and useful to teach… so that the servant of God may be thoroughly equipped." (2 Timothy 3:16-17, NLT)

You may not "win" the debate, but God promises His Word will never return void (Isaiah 55:11). You plant the seed, He makes it grow (1 Corinthians 3:6-8).

C. How to Break the Cycle

Mormon beliefs often shift with leadership changes. What's considered revelation one year may change the next. For example, in 2012, the LDS Church lowered the missionary age for women from 21 to 19, a rule reversal presented as "God's new direction." But in Christianity, God's truth is unchanging. His commandments are summarized in two:

1. Love God with all your heart, soul, and mind.
2. Love your neighbor as yourself (Matthew 22:37-39).

God's Word cannot be altered. "If anyone adds to these things, God will add to him the plagues written in this book" (Revelation 22:18, NLT).

D. A Personal Prayer

"Oh Lord, bless the one reading this. Fill them with courage and boldness, not self-reliance, but a heart that serves and depends fully on You. Remind them that as they open their mouths, Your Holy Spirit will speak through them. You are all-powerful, all-encompassing, and sovereign over every heart. Show them the faces and places where You are sending them. Put specific people, especially those lost in deception, on their hearts to pray for and to reach.

Strengthen them, Lord, for the joy of the Lord is their strength. Give them divine strategy and wisdom, for You are sending them out as sheep among wolves. Let their confidence rest in You alone. Break off deception Lord In The Name Of Jesus, Amen."

E. Media Missionaries

God has given us a new mission field, social media. What would Paul have done with an Instagram account? Every letter would've gone viral!

If you see a Mormon online, you'll notice their bio often includes a verse from the Book of Mormon or a link to mormon.org. Message them. Pray for them. You can plant a seed with a single text. They may not receive it, but your obedience still matters.

Mormons give themselves credit when they bring somebody into Mormonism, with their Mormon scripture: *Doctrine and Covenants 18:16, "And now, if your joy will be great with one soul that you have brought unto me into the kingdom of my Father, how great will be your joy if you should bring many souls unto me!"* This is in direct contrast to Biblical Scripture: John 6:44 NLT "For no one can come to me unless the Father who sent me draws them; and at the last day I will raise them up."

We, as Christian Evangelists, are to plant seed. God will send somebody ELSE to water that seed for you, and HE ALONE MAKES THE INCREASE! (1 Corinthians 3:6)

Go on, Soldier!

"The King will reply, 'Truly I tell you, whatever you did for one of the least of these... you did for me.'" (Matthew 25:40, NLT)

QUICK AND EASY FACT CHECK

Christianity and Mormonism share some language similarities, but their core teachings about God, salvation, and human destiny differ dramatically. The following outlines some of the largest differences:

1. Nature of God and the Trinity

- Christianity: God is one being in three coequal and coeternal persons, Father, Son, and Holy Spirit (Matthew 28:19, NLT).
- *Mormonism: God the Father, Jesus Christ, and the Holy Ghost are distinct beings. God is a literal, embodied father; Jesus and the Spirit are separate substances with distinct roles (Doctrine and Covenants 130:22).*

2. Jesus Christ

- Christianity: Jesus is fully God and fully man, whose death and resurrection provide complete salvation (John 3:16, NLT).
- *Mormonism: Jesus is the firstborn spirit child of God. Salvation depends on faith in Him plus obedience, baptism, temple ordinances, and following modern prophets (Book of Mormon, 2 Nephi 2:7).*

3. Scripture

- Christianity: The Bible alone is the inspired, authoritative Word of God.

- *Mormonism: Scripture includes the Bible, Book of Mormon, Doctrine & Covenants, and Pearl of Great Price (Book of Mormon Introduction).*

4. Prophets

- Christianity: Revelation was completed through Christ and the apostles; no new prophets are recognized.
- *Mormonism: Joseph Smith is regarded as a prophet who restored the true church and received modern revelation (Doctrine and Covenants 21:1).*

5. Salvation and Afterlife

- Christianity: Salvation is by faith in Christ alone; eternal life is a gift (Ephesians 2:8–9, NLT).
- *Mormonism: Salvation requires faith and works, ordinances, and obedience. Heaven is divided into celestial, terrestrial, and telestial kingdoms (Doctrine and Covenants 76).*

6. Authority and Priesthood

- Christianity: All believers have direct access to God through Christ (1 Peter 2:9, NLT).
- *Mormonism: A restored priesthood hierarchy is required for ordinances and spiritual authority (Doctrine and Covenants 13).*

7. Eternal Progression

- Christianity: Humans cannot become God; eternal life is a gift of grace.
- *Mormonism: Faithful men can progress to godhood; women can be exalted but are*

dependent on a righteous husband (Doctrine and Covenants 132).

8. Revelation

- Christianity: Divine revelation concluded with the apostles; some denominations allow interpretive guidance, but God's Word is complete.
- *Mormonism: God continues to reveal new doctrines through modern prophets (Doctrine and Covenants 1:38).*

9. Baptism

- Christianity: Baptism symbolizes faith in Christ; it is not a requirement to earn salvation (Romans 6:4, NLT).
- *Mormonism: Baptism by immersion is essential, including baptism for the dead (Book of Mormon, Mosiah 18:10).*

10. Heaven and Hell

- Christianity: Eternal life with God or separation from Him; some traditions include purgatory.
- *Mormonism: Three kingdoms of glory and outer darkness; placement depends on obedience and acceptance of the Gospel (Doctrine and Covenants 76).*

PARALLEL NAMES FROM BOOK OF MORMON TAKEN FROM THE BIBLE

Bible—King Lemuel is a ruler who wrote the first nine verses in Proverbs 31. He writes poetic advice from his mother. She warns him to abstain from women who are adulterers and says drunk rulers are not wise rulers.

Mormonism—Lemuel is Lehi's firstborn son who rejected the teachings of his father and persecuted and beat his brothers. His descendants became known as Lemuelites (1 Nephi 3, 7, 16, 18).

Bible—Amon is a wicked king from the Southern Kingdom who worshipped idols and was later assassinated (2 Kings 21:21).

Mormonism—Ammon was a Nephite missionary who gained fame by cutting off the arms of the Lamanite king's enemies (Alma 17:36).

Bible—-Laban is Jacob's mother's (Rebekah's) brother. (Genesis 29:10). He was an idolater. His daughters are Leah and Rachel, whom Jacob later fell in love with.

Mormonism—-Laban is the keeper of the brass plates whom Nephi later was told by mormon god to cut off the head of to obtain. (1 Nephi 3:12)

Bible—Jesus is God wrapped in human flesh who willingly came to sacrifice himself for the sins of the whole world.

Mormonism—Jesus is a very kind and nice man and the literal son of the Heavenly Father who suffered to gain his own salvation. He made a way for Mormons to do the same, to gain their salvation and exaltation (become a god someday) (Doctrine & Covenants

*93:12-14+76:58+132:20; Teachings of the Prophet
Joseph Smith, p. 392).*

Bible— Holy Spirit is Another Comforter, who
brings all things to your remembrance and intercedes on
your behalf in prayer. He never leaves you nor forsakes
you.

*Mormonism— Holy Spirit is a comforter, like a
blanket, who is there with you as long as you are choosing
the right. The Holy Ghost cannot dwell with you when you
make wrong decisions and can flee (Doctrine & Covenants
97:17+121:37; Gospel Principles, ch. 7, "The Holy
Ghost)*

Bible—Satan is a fallen angel who fell like
lightning from Heaven when he disobeyed the father and
wanted the Glory for himself. He was made as a beautiful
and musical angel with instruments built into his body.
When he wanted the glory for himself he was cast down
from heaven. He is walking to and fro on the earth and has
a time clock. He was defeated when Jesus said "IT IS
FINISHED." Satan blinds the minds of unbelievers to
bring them down to Hell. God has given his children
authority over all the power of the enemy.

*Mormonism— Satan is Jesus's brother. The second
one to volunteer after Jesus when God asked who he
should send into the world. He is the serpent who deceived
Eve. Acts as a friend to tempt mormons to leave their
families and their one true church (Doctrine & Covenants
93; Abraham 3).*

Bible—- Jared was a biblical patriarch who lived
before the Great Flood and is mentioned in the genealogies
of Genesis 5 and Luke 3. He was the son of Mahalaleel
and father of Enoch. He was the second oldest man in the
Bible and lived to be 962 years. Jared lived to see the
death of Adam, the birth of Noah, and the early life of
Noah's three sons. There are no Jaredites mentioned in the
Bible. (Genesis 5:15)

Bible—-The Amalekites are a formidable tribe of
nomads (wanderers) living in the area south of Canaan
between Mount Seir and the Egyptian border. They were
descendants of Amalek, the grandson of Esau. They
resisted the Israelites and remained perennial foes of God's
people and hated the Jews. They did not originate until
after Esau's time. They were threats to God's people many
times (Moses's people during the Exodus, Hormah,
David's wives at Ziklag + children, etc) and the last we
hear about them is in the book of Esther where the rest of
Israel's enemies were destroyed.

Bible—-Levi/Levites- the third son of Jacob and
Leah, both a man and a tribe. Levi's anger was evil
because it was characterized by deeds of fierceness and
cruelty such as a violent destruction of the Schechemites
(this deed included his brother Simeon). The tribe of Levi
was scattered through Israel. But they became, by God's
grace and through their loyalty to God, the priestly tribe
and residents of the cities of refuge. The other tribes of
Israel received a land inheritance in Canaan, but the
Levites received no land. The Levites' inheritance was
God himself, tithes, and cities.

years in jail before overthrowing the king of the Jaredites (Ether 10).

Bible—-Korah is the son of Izhar, a Levite whose blatant rebellion against Moses and Aaron brought about his own demise as well as the deaths of everyone aligned with him. After they revolted against the authority of Moses and Aaron in the wilderness, Korah's story illustrates a vital truth about the seriousness of sin and rebellion against God's chosen leaders. (Numbers 16)

Mormonism—-Korihor was an AntiChrist in the Book of Mormon who didn't believe in the afterlife. He was an apostate teacher and later lost his voice as a sign from their god and was later begging for food and killed (Alma 30).

PARALLEL STORIES BIBLE VS BOOK OF MORMON

(The Bible was written 3,000+ years before the Book of Mormon ever came about, and Joseph Smith had a Bible in hand)

Mormons often highlight similarities between the Book of Mormon and the Bible, believing these parallels confirm the truth of their scripture. What they don't realize is that the Bible warns against any altered or rival gospel (Galatians 1:6–9). Below are the similar names and storylines, listed first are the similar names, followed by the biblical narratives that Joseph Smith replicated and reassigned under different characters in the Book of Mormon.

KING AHAB VS KING NOAH

Bible—-<u>King Ahab</u> ruled the northern kingdom of Israel and is remembered as one of its most wicked kings. He lived in luxury, building ivory palaces and surrounding himself with excess. Influenced heavily by his wife Jezebel, he promoted idolatry, murdered God's prophets, and openly opposed the Lord. The prophet Elijah confronted him, warning of judgment, disaster, and famine. Ahab refused to listen and ultimately died in battle, just as the prophet had warned (1 Kings 16, 18, 22).

Mormonism—-<u>King Noah</u> led his people into idolatry and corruption, supported by a group of wicked priests who avoided all accountability. He taxed the people heavily to support his extravagant lifestyle and built lavish structures for his own glory. He persecuted anyone who *tried to live righteously. The prophet Abinadi boldly confronted Noah, prophesying destruction and coming bondage. Enraged, Noah ordered Abinadi to be burned alive. In the end, Noah himself was killed by his own people—fulfilling Abinadi's prophecy exactly (Mosiah 11, 17).*

SAUL VS *ALMA THE YOUNGER*

Bible—- shows true conversion through <u>Saul's</u> encounter with the risen Christ. A light from heaven knocked him to the ground, Jesus spoke to him, and he was blinded for three days (Acts 9:3–9, NLT). When his sight was restored, he was filled with the Holy Spirit and immediately began preaching Jesus as Lord (Acts 9:17–20, NLT). His entire life redirected toward the gospel.

The Book of Mormon presents <u>Alma the Younger</u> in a strikingly similar pattern. He is confronted by an angel, collapses, loses his strength, remembers his sins, and then rises claiming conversion (Mosiah 27:11–32). But instead of proclaiming Christ according to Scripture, Alma devotes himself to promoting the LDS church.

JOSEPH OF EGYPT VS *NEPHI*

Bible—- <u>Joseph of Egypt</u> is a young son favored by God (Genesis 37). He receives visions and prophetic dreams, and his brothers resent him. Joseph is sent by his father Jacob to check on his brothers and obeys without murmuring. Because of jealousy, his brothers hate him for receiving revelation and even attempt to kill him. They reject his spiritual insight. God delivers Joseph from the pit and from slavery, remaining with him and ultimately using him to preserve his family. Joseph rises to power in Egypt and becomes a ruler and guide for his family, his brothers eventually bow before him. He interprets dreams and preserves important records in Egypt, becoming a keeper of wisdom. Through him, God preserves His covenant people, and the Lord makes everything he does prosper (Genesis 39:3).

Mormonism—-<u>Nephi</u> is likewise a young son favored by God, described as "highly favored of the Lord" (1 Nephi 1:1). He receives visions and prophetic dreams, and his older brothers resent him. They reject spiritual insight and call visions "foolish." Nephi is delivered from danger repeatedly, and God is with him (1 Nephi 7:17), using him to preserve his family.

Nephi eventually becomes the spiritual and political leader of his people (2 Nephi 5), and his brothers, at least those who choose righteousness, end up following him.

PAUL AND SILAS VS *ALMA AND AMULEK*

Bible—-<u>Paul and Silas</u> are powerful Christian missionaries whose preaching in Philippi angers corrupt leaders. These men stir up the crowd, resulting in Paul and Silas being beaten and thrown into the deepest part of the prison with their feet in stocks. During the night, a violent earthquake shakes the prison, opening the doors and loosening their chains. The jailer, witnessing the miracle, believes in the Lord, and he and his entire household are converted (Acts 16).

Mormonism—-<u>Alma and Amulek</u> preach repentance to the people of Ammonihah, provoking the anger of corrupt lawyers and judges. They are mocked, starved, abused, and imprisoned. As they cry out to God, the prison shakes violently, the walls collapse, and their *captors are killed—while Alma and Amulek walk out unharmed. Afterward, Zeezrom repents and becomes a faithful missionary because of what he witnessed (Alma 10, 14, 15).*

KORAH VS *SHEREM*

Bible—-<u>Korah</u> was persuasive and publicly opposes God's appointed leader Moses and denies the authority of the prophet. He leads people astray and demands to be acknowledged as right. He asks for proof and is dramatically judged by God. His downfall is used as a warning for the people (Numbers 16).

Mormonism—-<u>Sherem</u> was a persuasive and powerful speaker who led people astray by teaching against Christ and denying the coming Messiah. He confronted Jacob and demanded a sign, but God struck him down because of his pride. Before dying, Sherem confessed that he had been deceived by the devil and wrong to oppose the truth. His death served as a sobering warning to the Nephites (Jacob 7).

JESUS'S SERMON ON THE MOUNT VS *KING BENJAMIN'S SPEECH*

Bible—-<u>Jesus</u>, fully God and fully man, spoke from an elevated mountain so the people could hear Him. Large crowds gathered to hear Jesus teach. There He delivered a message that called His followers to a transformed heart, one that hungers for righteousness, loves its enemies, walks in humility, practices forgiveness, and trusts in God's provision.

Mormonism—-<u>King Benjamin</u>, the final Nephite king in Zarahemla, is portrayed as a righteous and wise leader whose reign brought peace and spiritual renewal. He built a tower so the people could hear him, and families camped around the temple to receive his message.

EXODUS OF THE ISRAELITES VS EXODUS OF *LEHI'S FAMILY*

Bible—-Exodus of the Israelites: A pivotal moment in the Old Testament where Moses leads the Israelites out of bondage in Egypt and into the wilderness, guided by God's hand.

Mormonism—- The Exodus of Lehi's Family (1 Nephi 2)
Lehi's family is led out of Jerusalem by God to flee from impending destruction. They travel into the wilderness, relying on God's guidance.

JEREMIAH VS *LEHI*

Bible—-<u>Jeremiah</u> was called by God as a prophet around 626 BCE during the reign of King Josiah, and he continued his prophetic ministry through the final destruction of Jerusalem in 586 BCE. He is known as the weeping prophet and his primary message was one of warning, urging the people of Judah to repent from their idolatry and wickedness and return to the worship of the true God. He foretold the coming destruction of Jerusalem and the Babylonian exile, which occurred during the reign of King Zedekiah, the last king of Judah. Zephaniah, Habakkuk, and Ezekiel all were prophets who warned the destruction of Jerusalem as well.

Mormonism- The Book of Mormon presents <u>Lehi</u> in a strikingly similar pattern. Lehi Warns Jerusalem and was called by the "lord" to prophesy about the impending destruction of Jerusalem, which was due to the people's wickedness particularly in response to the actions of King

Zedekiah, Hezekiah's son. Lehi departs Jerusalem shortly before its destruction around 600 BCE.

SHADRACH MESHACH AND ABEDNEGO VS NEPHI AND LEHI

Bible— <u>Shadrach, Meshach, and Abednego</u> are Hebrew men living under King Nebuchadnezzar in Babylon. They are commanded to bow to a golden image, but they refuse to worship idols. The king throws them into a fiery furnace, yet the fire does not harm them. A fourth figure appears in the flames "like a son of God," and they walk out completely unharmed—their clothes not even smelling like smoke. The king witnesses the miracle and praises the Lord (Daniel 3).

Mormonism—- <u>Nephi and Lehi</u>, the sons of Helaman, are preaching repentance to the Lamanites when they are cast into prison. As prisoners threaten them, a pillar of fire surrounds them but does not burn them. A heavenly voice speaks three times, and a great earthquake shakes the prison. The Lamanites are filled with fear, cry out for mercy, and many repent as they witness the miracle (Helaman 5:22–52).

NOAH'S ARK VS *BROTHER OF JARED AND NEPHI*

Bible—- God commands <u>Noah</u>, a righteous man, to build an ark (Genesis 6–9). God gives very specific instructions—a rectangular structure with one door, one window, and completely sealed with pitch. The waters rise, the earth is covered, it rains for 40 days, and the deep fountains burst forth. The ark is tossed but secure, and Noah remains inside for about a year. God preserves the righteous through judgment, and Noah's ark is unlike anything ever seen.

Mormonism—-In the Book of Mormon, the <u>Brother of Jared</u> is likewise instructed by God to build barges (Ether 2–6). The instructions include making them tight like a dish, sealed on top and bottom, with a hole in the top and a hole in the bottom for ventilation, and covered with pitch. God touches stones to give the barges light, and a furious wind drives them across the ocean. They face mountain waves, storms, and being buried in the depths, yet they are preserved. The journey lasts 344 days, and God leads the righteous through trials toward a promised land.

Mormonism—-A third parallel appears in the Book of Mormon with <u>Nephi</u>, who also receives a direct command from God to build a ship (1 Nephi 17–18). He is instructed to build it "not after the manner of men," but according to divine design. God teaches him step by step, and while his brothers Laman and Lemuel mock and oppose him, Nephi remains obedient. His ship ultimately carries his family safely across the great waters.

<u>URIM AND THUMMIM</u>

Bible—the <u>Urim and Thummim</u> were sacred objects placed in the high priest's breastplate (Exodus 28:30) and used to discern God's will, likely in limited, decision-based ways. They were tied specifically to the Levitical priesthood and Israel's covenant system, not to private revelation or translating texts. Scripture gives very little detail about their form and shows their use **fading** after the early Old Testament period.

Mormonism—The Book of Mormon describes the "<u>Urim and Thummim</u>" as interpreters: seer stones set in a frame, used by Joseph Smith to translate the golden plates. This usage expands the concept significantly, portraying *them as instruments for receiving and transmitting lengthy revelatory texts, rather than making limited priestly inquiries. Additionally, the Book of Mormon tradition blends the term with other seer stones, making the definition broader and less tied to the Old Testament priesthood context.*

There are many more similarities/parallels such as: THE SERMON ON THE MOUNT (Matthew 5-7) VS *THE SERMON AT THE TEMPLE (3 Nephi 12-14)=* Verbatim copying of KJV text, despite being set in the Americas—- JESUS CALMING THE STORM (Matthew 8) VS *NEPHI CALMING THE STORM (1 Nephi 18)* Focus is on Nephi rather than Jesus---- JESUS CHOOSING TWELVE APOSTLES (Matthew 10) VS *JESUS CHOOSING TWELVE NEPHITE DISCIPLES (3 Nephi 12)*---- THE TOWER OF BABEL LANGUAGE CONFUSION VS *THE BROTHER OF JARED'S LANGUAGE PRESERVED (Ether 1)* —- BREAKING BREAD & THE EUCHARIST (Matthew 26) *VS NEPHITE SACRAMENT PRAYERS (Moroni 4-5)* —- THE FALL OF JERUSALEM (Matthew 24) *VS THE FALL OF THE NEPHITES/JAREDITES (Mormon & Ether).*

SEE FULL CHAPTER in "From Mormon To God Book 2 QUICK FACT CHECK PAMPHLET" available on Amazon.

ANACHRONISMS

An anachronism occurs when an object, practice, or technology appears in a historical account before it existed in that time or place. When a sacred text presents itself as historical, archaeology becomes one way, though not the only way, to examine how its claims align with the world in which they are said to have occurred.

Biblical Archaeological Harmony

The Bible situates its narrative within real places, rulers, and cultures. Over time, archaeology has repeatedly illuminated this historical setting. Figures once questioned, such as King David, have moved from uncertainty to historical recognition through discoveries like the Tel Dan Stele, which refers to the "House of David." Peoples such as the Hittites, once thought to exist only in Scripture, are now well documented through inscriptions, archives, and city remains throughout the ancient Near East.

Locations described in the Bible have likewise come into clearer focus. The Pool of Siloam, mentioned in the Gospel of John, has been uncovered in Jerusalem in a form consistent with first-century descriptions (John 9:7, NLT). Assyrian records align closely with biblical accounts of kings such as Hezekiah and events such as Sennacherib's campaign against Judah, offering parallel testimony from outside the biblical text (2 Kings 18–19, NLT).

Perhaps most striking is the preservation of Scripture itself. The Dead Sea Scrolls, copied centuries before Christ, show that the Hebrew Scriptures were transmitted with remarkable care. While archaeology does not prove theology, it has repeatedly shown the Bible to be historically anchored in the world it describes. Discoveries have tended not to overturn biblical claims, but rather to clarify and, in many cases, confirm them.

Book of Mormon Historical Tensions

The Book of Mormon also presents itself as a historical record, describing ancient civilizations in the Americas between approximately 2200 BC and AD 421. Within this narrative, familiar Old World elements appear: animals, materials, and technologies that invite careful examination when placed alongside what is currently known of ancient American history.

The text refers to horses, cattle, sheep, goats, swine, and even elephants as part of the lived environment (1 Nephi 18:25; Ether 9:18–19). Yet archaeological and paleontological evidence indicates that these animals were either absent from the Americas during the proposed time period or had become extinct long before. Similarly, references to iron and steel, wheeled transport, and chariots suggest technologies that, if present at scale, would be expected to leave material traces, though such evidence has not been found.

Agricultural and luxury items such as wheat and silk are also mentioned, despite being Old World resources not known to have existed in pre-Columbian American societies. One item, barley, was long considered an anachronism and later shown to have existed in limited form. While this adjustment refines one point, it does not resolve the broader pattern of materials and technologies that remain historically unaccounted for within the Book of Mormon's setting.

For readers who value historical continuity, these questions are not raised to diminish faith, but to acknowledge the difference between texts whose historical claims have steadily aligned with external evidence and those whose material culture remains largely uncorroborated. The contrast invites reflection, patience, and thoughtful engagement rather than haste or dismissal.

CONCLUSION OF BOOK 2

I'm deeply grateful and honored to have the assignment to share what I believe is truth with those in the Mormon community, and to help Christian evangelists better understand Mormon beliefs so they can lovingly reach others and make disciples of all nations, as the Bible teaches.

I'll officially end this book just as I did book one with a quote from Walter Martin, Christian Theologist - "I want to teach the truth. I don't want to make mistakes. I am responsible for mistakes that you make if you believe what I say. But so are you if you believe what I say without checking what God said. There is a dual-responsibility. Where I'm consistent with scripture, obey! Where I'm not, correct me! Because it's terribly important that the body of Christ gets sound doctrine, and you cannot get sound doctrine with corrupt methods of interpretation. Impossible… That's why hermeneutics is important, this word translates to "making sure". Make sure what you tell somebody is really what God said… If you walk out of this room this morning and say, "Walter Martin says", you could be wrong, I'm fallible, I make mistakes just like everybody else. We all make mistakes. We all make misinterpretations. We all fail somewhere and I'm a teacher, I'm more held responsible for this than you are! That's what James tells me… Get your instruction from somebody, faithful to the word of God, with the authority to teach within the body of Christ. It doesn't rest on what I think or what I say… It rests on whether or not it corresponds with (biblical) scripture!"

Other great resources: CES LETTER

+   SEE FULL CHAPTER in "From Mormon To God
    Book 2 QUICK FACT CHECK PAMPHLET"
    available on Amazon.

END
WWW. FROMMORMONTOGOD.COM

Biography

Kristen Hale grew up in a Mormon family of nine. She followed the rules and ordinances of the Mormon faith, but when come down with a life-threatening and life-altering illness, God picked her up in His grace and she said a quick goodbye to her old belief system. She was once lost, and now found. Once ill, and now healed COMPLETELY by Jesus. She is now a member of a nondenominational Christian believers' church Restoration Ministries in Visalia, California, where she assists in worship. She lives with her husband and three kids.

Kristen has a certificate in advanced-level psychology, an associate's degree in science from Utah State University, a Bachelor's degree in piano performance from the University of Utah, a Master's degree in Theology from Golden Grain Bible College, and a one-way ticket into God's kingdom through God's only perfect son Jesus Christ.

WORKS CITED

Bibles & Biblical Study Resources

Bible Hub. (n.d.). Bible Hub: Search, read, study the Bible in many languages. https://biblehub.com

Blue Letter Bible. (n.d.). Blue Letter Bible: Study tools. https://www.blueletterbible.org

Crossway Bibles. (2016). The Holy Bible: English Standard Version. Crossway.

Tyndale House Publishers. (2015). Holy Bible: New Living Translation. Tyndale House.

Zondervan. (2020). The NIV study Bible (Fully revised ed.). Zondervan.

Christian Books, Theology, and Apologetics

Brown, D. (2023). How to read the Bible for all its worth. Zondervan.

Burge, G. M. (2020). The New Testament in antiquity (2nd ed.). Zondervan.

Busenitz, N. (2015). Long before Luther: Tracing the heart of the gospel from Christ to the Reformation. Moody Publishers.

Calvin, J. (2009). Institutes of the Christian religion (H. Beveridge, Trans.). Hendrickson Publishers. (Original work published 1536)

Domeris, W. R. (2014). Jesus on trial: A study guide. Cascade Books.

Fee, G. D., & Stuart, D. (2014). How to read the Bible for all its worth (4th ed.). Zondervan.

Geisler, N. (2011). Systematic theology (Vols. 1–4). Bethany House.

Grudem, W. (1994). Christian beliefs: Twenty basics every Christian should know. Zondervan.

Grudem, W. (2020). Systematic theology (2nd ed.). Zondervan Academic.

MacArthur, J. (2008). The truth war: Fighting for certainty in an age of deception. Thomas Nelson.

MacArthur, J. (2020). Biblical doctrine: A systematic summary of Bible truth. Crossway.

Mounce, W. D. (2006). Basics of biblical Greek: Grammar (3rd ed.). Zondervan.

Sproul, R. C. (2000). Chosen by God. Tyndale House.

Sproul, R. C. (2016). Everyone's a theologian: An introduction to systematic theology. Reformation Trust Publishing.

Official LDS Scriptures & Documents

Joseph Smith Jr. (Trans.). (1830/1981). The Book of Mormon: Another testament of Jesus Christ. The Church of Jesus Christ of Latter-day Saints.

Joseph Smith Jr. (1835/1981). Doctrine and Covenants. The Church of Jesus Christ of Latter-day Saints.

Joseph Smith Jr. (1842/1981). The Pearl of Great Price. The Church of Jesus Christ of Latter-day Saints.

The Church of Jesus Christ of Latter-day Saints. (1995). The family: A proclamation to the world. Author.

LDS Manuals, Articles & Online Sources

Book of Mormon Central. (n.d.). Archive & study resources. https://bookofmormoncentral.org

BYU Studies. (n.d.). BYU Studies Quarterly. https://byustudies.byu.edu

Deseret News. (n.d.). https://www.deseret.com

Ensign Magazine. (n.d.). Ensign (LDS Magazine Archive). https://www.churchofjesuschrist.org/study/ensign

LDS Living. (n.d.). LDS Living Magazine. https://www.ldsliving.com

The Church News. (n.d.). https://www.thechurchnews.com

Christian Websites, Ministries & Online References

BibleStudyTools. (n.d.). https://www.biblestudytools.com

CARM. (n.d.). Christian Apologetics & Research Ministry. https://carm.org

Christianity Today. (n.d.). https://www.christianitytoday.com

Desiring God. (n.d.). https://www.desiringgod.org

GotQuestions Ministries. (n.d.). Got Questions? Biblical answers. https://www.gotquestions.org

Grace to You. (n.d.). John MacArthur's Bible teaching ministry. https://www.gty.org

Ligonier Ministries. (n.d.). https://www.ligonier.org

Monergism. (n.d.). Theology & Bible study library. https://www.monergism.com

The Gospel Coalition. (n.d.). https://www.thegospelcoalition.org

---

YouTube, Audio & Sermon Sources

Grace to You. (n.d.). YouTube Channel. https://www.youtube.com/user/GraceToYou

The Bible Project. (n.d.). Videos on biblical themes. https://www.youtube.com/user/jointhebibleproject

The Gospel Coalition. (n.d.). YouTube Channel. https://www.youtube.com/user/TGCresources

---

Historical, Dictionary, and General Reference Sources

Britannica. (n.d.). Encyclopedia Britannica Online. https://www.britannica.com

Merriam-Webster. (n.d.). Merriam-Webster Dictionary. https://www.merriam-webster.com

Oxford University Press. (n.d.). Oxford Reference. https://www.oxfordreference.com

Wikipedia. (n.d.). Wikipedia: The Free Encyclopedia.
https://www.wikipedia.org

Additional sources:

Holy Bible, New Living Translation. (1996). Tyndale
House Publishers.

The Church of Jesus Christ of Latter-day Saints. (1981).
The Book of Mormon: Another Testament of Jesus Christ.
Salt Lake City, UT.

The Church of Jesus Christ of Latter-day Saints. (n.d.).
Doctrine and Covenants. Salt Lake City, UT.

Dever, W. G. (2001). What Did the Biblical Writers Know
and When Did They Know It? Eerdmans.

Kitchen, K. A. (2003). On the Reliability of the Old
Testament. Eerdmans.

Price, R. (2003). The Stones Cry Out: What Archaeology
Reveals About the Truth of the Bible. Harvest House.